LEEDS THROUGH A LENS

THE INSIDE STORY OF A REMARKABLE SEASON

Words by Paul Dews

Acknowledgements

This book couldn't have been produced without the help and support of... Ken Bates, Shaun Harvey, Dennis Wise, Gary McAllister, the players of Leeds United, the staff of Leeds United, and the many thousands of fans of this great club. Without all of you, this wouldn't be half the story that it is.

Credits

Thanks to Neil Jeffries, Trevor Hartley, Ian Guildford, Andrew Varley, Don Warters, Stix Lockwood, PA Photos, Action Images and to all of you who supplied pictures to the matchday programme throughout the season.

Also a big thanks to Steve Parkin and Clipper Logistics who kindly agreed to sponsor the publication.

First published in the United Kingdom by Leeds United Football Club in 2008.

ISBN 978-0-9560675-0-0

Printed and bound by Pureprint Group.

CONTENTS

FOREWORD

By Ken Bates

When a future researcher comes to write an official record of Leeds United he, or she, will probably choose the season 2007/08 as the turning point in the history of this troubled club, when it shook off the last vestige of its turbulent past and started the long road back to where it should belong.

January 2007 was beginning to look promising. On the pitch Leeds were struggling but Wisey was confident that the team would stay up. Off the pitch, on the financial side, things were looking good. The previous autumn, through a contact of mine in Monte Carlo, we had been negotiating with an Irish consortium to invest in the club and matters were drawing to completion. At the same time we had reached an agreement with JJB Sports to take over the running of our retail business for five years on a royalty basis with a guaranteed minimum of £5.5 million over the period. The slight niggle was our inability to launch season ticket renewals owing to the uncertainty of our league position. All clubs, except the rich few, rely on season ticket renewals to help their cash flow through the spring and summer.

At the time the Irish deal was a good one – £10 million investment in the club in return for 25 per cent of the shares; a 20-year £20 million loan to buy back the freehold of both Elland Road and the training ground; and a promise of the finance needed to redevelop the land behind the East Stand which would bring vital commercial income not dependent on results on the pitch.

The culmination of the two years of hard work would mean we could clear the inherited Revenue arrears, own the freehold, replace the rent with lower interest payments and have working capital and funds for the team.

Then the thunderbolt struck. George Canning, representing the Irish consortium, telephoned. He explained that he had received a telephone call from Melvyn Levi, the former Leeds director, who had made certain representations and allegations against me (all of which were totally false). Until the matter was cleared up they would withdraw from the deal. As I was contemplating this setback, Yvonne Todd, the club's Finance Director, entered the room to tell me that JJB Sports was insisting we terminated our existing contract before they signed the new deal. In the absence of a new deal, we could not take the risk of buying out the old one. In one hour I had lost £15.5 million of new finance. Recovering quickly, we pursued other suitors, all of which came to a juddering halt when, out of the blue, Gerald Krasner, the former chairman of the board which had aggravated the mess left by Ridsdale, went on TV to forecast that Leeds would go into administration shortly and that the club would be saved by a new consortium (headed by Simon Morris) which was waiting in the wings.

Faced with this turn of events, which effectively killed off any chance of further investors, the board sought professional advice from solicitors Walker Morris who in turn introduced us to KPMG, one of the top four insolvency partnerships in the country. When many companies, unfortunately, go into administration they continue trading. They have book debts, stock, order books and work in progress which provide the funds to keep the business ticking over, pending reorganisation and hopefully sale. Football clubs are not like that. When they are in trouble, they have no money and their biggest expense is to pay the players' wages immediately. Furthermore, an administrator is not allowed to take risks or borrow money. The only solution was what is known as a pre-pack, whereby the club is put into administration and immediately sold on. This is what happened in the case of Leeds. It needed approval by 75 per cent of the unsecured creditors and subsequently this was achieved on Friday June 1 when the creditors voted 75.2 per cent in favour. Much was made of the narrowness of the margin, particularly by Lord Mawhinney, chairman of the Football League, who forgot to mention that at his instigation the League itself voted against the CVA. However, 75 per cent is 75 per cent. The administrators sold both the Retail, Conference & Banqueting part of the business to the ultimate new owners, thus ensuring they continued trading (at a loss of £863,000 up to and including June 30, 2007).

The law provides that following the creditors meeting there is a period of 28 days for any dissatisfied creditors to appeal to the High Court. At 4pm on the 28th day, the Inland Revenue appealed. At the High Court the appeal was expected to be heard within a day or two, instead the judge set a date in September. Pandemonium ensued – there was no money available to keep the club going. Up until that point, the would-be owners had been funding the administrators but refused to do so for a further two months, only to possibly see the club fold or sold to another party. Furthermore, the Revenue indicated that if they lost in September, they could appeal again.

Behind the scenes, somebody was pulling the strings of three MPs – Phil Willis (Lib Dem) of Harrogate & Knaresborough, Colin Burgon (Labour) of Elmet and George Mudie (Labour) of Leeds East. I had never heard of any of them and I had certainly never met them. They became very vocal making statements to the media and putting down an Early Day Motion in the Houses of Parliament (a welcome respite no doubt from the wearisome task of filling in their expense claim forms).

KPMG then offered the club to anybody on a competitive basis. This attracted the same sort of time-wasters I had endured over my year at Leeds. Most prominent was our old friend Simon Morris who now appears to have troubles of his own elsewhere.

Things dragged on over the summer as the other contenders failed the put-up-or-shut-up test, or made their offers conditional. With time running out, the current owners took a calculated risk, making their offer unconditional and thereby taking on the risk that Leeds would not be readmitted to the Football League following the withdrawal of their membership upon administration. Meanwhile the aggravation continued in the media. Gerald Krasner got involved with the Supporters Club, whose chairman Ray Fell had to make a public apology to me for a statement he made. The fringe players squealed and stamped their feet but the noise gradually lessened and they faded away.

Slowly, the atmosphere became more positive around the city. All the staff, both at Elland Road and Thorp Arch, worked beyond the call of duty throughout this turbulent time, not knowing whether they would get paid or even have a job at the end of it.

On the playing side it was more difficult. Unable to sign new players or renew existing contracts until our league membership was confirmed, Dennis Wise was suffering. He and Technical Director Gwyn Williams had lined up a list of players who were available on 'Bosman' free transfers and had agreed to join Leeds. However, with all the uncertainty they began to drift away to other clubs. They, too, had mortgages to pay and mouths to feed. However, Dennis and Gus kept up the morale of all around them while waiting for a resolution of the problem. Dennis Wise kept some of the players happy by helping them out of his own pocket, quietly and without any publicity, we subsequently found out.

The Football League continued to prevaricate, always requesting we send them yet another piece of information, and slating KPMG for being unhelpful. For their part KPMG pointed out that they consulted their lawyers Walker Morris, together with two independent QCs, at every step of the way. Finally on Friday August 3, just five working days before the start of the season we heard their decision. Readmitted, subject to a 15-point penalty with the right of appeal to all Member Clubs of the Football League on the following Thursday. This 'kangaroo court' was duly convened and it rubber-stamped the FL board's decision. Meanwhile, there was a mad rush to register contracts, sign players and leave for Tranmere where we stuffed the b******s with a late winner.

Leeds United were back in business.

msterdam · Belfast · Düsseldorf · Paris
Jet2.com
Great to come home to

LIFE MUST GO ON

RAGGY ARSE ROVERS

It was an assorted bunch who gathered at Leeds Bradford Airport on the morning of Saturday July 7, 2007, for the first pre-season game at Shelbourne. The travelling party included no less than seven trialists and not one of the players boarding the plane had been paid for two months. The *Yorkshire Evening Post* newspaper accused the club of showing "scant regard for fans" by displaying squad news on the club website, but irrespective of events off the field, life had to go on, and there was a football season to prepare for.

'Raggy Arse Rovers' is a derogatory term in football parlance, used to describe a shoddy team or club, but the phrase proved sadly apt as Leeds United headed out to Ireland for that first game of the summer. RyanAir were reluctant to allow the kit on the plane due to weight restrictions and one peep inside the huge team skips carrying the kit revealed an odd-ball arrangement of the previous season's kit, long- and short-sleeved shirts, some bearing former sponsor logos, others with huge yellow patches covering those old designs.

The flight was delayed for over an hour and, on arrival, Robbie Blake – with his tongue in his cheek – described the hotel as "Fawlty Towers" and mused, "Is this how far we have fallen?" Yet, it was the first opportunity for the new squad to billet together and goals from Blake and David Prutton secured victory in front of almost five thousand fans, the majority sporting Leeds colours.

As a gesture, the club were presented with a plate to commemorate the game against our Irish friends, but in keeping with the theme of the moment,

while attempting to ensure all the kit was passed safely through Dublin airport check-in for the return journey, the said item was accidentally dropped on the terminal floor and damaged beyond repair.

AND THE WINNER IS...

Monday July 9 was billed as D-Day for the club with a 5pm deadline set by the administrators for potential bidders. Ken Bates had renewed his bid and, having taken advice, said firmly that he would mount a legal challenge if he failed to win control. Having agreed the purchase once, with the required creditor approval, the system had been thrown into farce by the actions of the Inland Revenue.

Shortly after 4pm it became clear that one group, Redbus, headed by London-based businessman Simon Franks, had tabled a bid. What emerged shortly afterwards was that Redbus had gone in with Simon Morris, a former director of the club. The media loved it. A "superbid" was trumpeted. Adam Pearson, another former director, who had recently been in the chair at Hull, was also thought to have made a bid, backed by fellow Leeds fan Peter Wilkinson, but no one knew for sure. KPMG, the administrators, weren't

Top: **The shirts for the game at Shelbourne didn't even match.**
Bottom: **A team at an Under-10s tournament in Nice watched by Chairman Ken Bates and his wife Suzannah (far left) were impeccably turned out.**

The club stall at the Great Yorkshire Show provided and opportunity for some bargain hunting, autographs from Shaun Derry and – at the end of the day – a rare treat for the staff working hard through times of great uncertainty.

Above: **Rui Marques, here in action at York, signed a contract extension...** *Right:* **...but David Healy had to be sold to Fulham.**

revealing any names and a simple statement said a decision would be made "in due course".

That "course" took almost 48 additional hours before it was announced that Ken Bates was the successful bidder. Joint administrator Richard Fleming confirmed: "We received several offers for the business which we considered carefully. The approved deal represents the best result for creditors in the circumstances and we believe provides the club with the best chance of survival."

It was during this period of uncertainty that the club took up residence at the Great Yorkshire Show in Harrogate. There were games, competitions, entertainment and Shaun Derry even popped in to demonstrate his ball skills. But the visitors to the club's stand were, understandably, far more interested in what the short and long-term future held for Leeds United.

It was anticipated that confirmation of the ownership of the club would result in the Football League agreeing to transfer the 'golden share' back to the new company, but nothing so straightforward happened. Instead, the Football League board requested "...from the administrators, certain required documentation and assurances regarding the sale of the club. The Board also requires certainty on the current legal proceedings surrounding the administration." The Football League board also "...expressed concern at the handling of the whole process by the administrators and the Chairman was instructed to obtain legal advice in that regard."

It was a statement which led to more doubt and confusion about whether or not the club would start the season at Tranmere in just four weeks time.

At the end of another "troubled week", Dennis Wise took his squad to York City for the second pre-season game. Wise used 22 players in the game, making wholesale changes throughout, and over two thousand Leeds fans watched a 0-0 draw. Once again, thoughts were diverted from the off-field situation, and there was some mild amusement when a number of fans capitalised on an absence of stewards on the away terrace to stage their own good-natured penalty shoot-out in the York goalmouth while the game was actually in play! A defiant Dennis Wise faced the media after the game, along with Eddie Lewis, and both were adamant that the management and players were being drawn even closer together.

With so much going on, it almost slipped by unnoticed that popular strikers David Healy and Robbie Blake had moved on ahead of the York City game. Healy joined Premier League Fulham and Blake returned to his former club Burnley.

C
F

WARMING UP... IN GERMANY

Club in turmoil? No League membership? No matter: we're Leeds and we're off to Germany. Trusting that there would be a season to prepare for, the club had three games lined up against Union Berlin, Dynamo Dresden and Energie Cottbus. The squad, again comprising a mixture of trialists and contracted players, headed for Berlin and a German heatwave. The training facilities on day one were on an pitch adjacent to Union Berlin's stadium and, perhaps forgetting that the opening game was only a few hours away, Dennis and the coaching staff put the players through the first of what proved to be a gruelling training schedule in Germany.

The Berlin game kicked off in the evening with temperatures still in the 20s and before a crowd of 16,000 in a somewhat frenzied atmosphere for a pre-season friendly. The home side ran out 2-1 winners and proceeded to celebrate as if they had won the Bundesliga. Amazing. The sizeable Leeds following departed with more disappointed faces. The manager, though, was unconcerned, citing fitness as his main priority. "It's nice to win games for the people that come out here," he observed. "But everything is geared up for August 11 and that's when it counts."

Next up came a trip to Dresden, two hours south of Berlin. The party would be staying in the Dresden suburb of Radebeul for the next few days, but

en route to the city it transpired that Saturday's friendly with Dynamo Dresden would probably be cancelled. On arrival at the hotel, Dennis Wise, Gus Poyet and Gwyn Williams were greeted by two Dresden officials and a member of the local constabulary who confirmed that Saturday's game would not take place because of fears about "a thousand potential troublemakers from Leeds attending the game". Further discussions revealed that there was a neo-nazi rally in neighbouring Leipzig on the same afternoon and the Dresden police would be drafted in to assist. Like the friendly, the rally had been planned for some weeks, but 48 hours before the game it transpired the local force were unable to police the game and Dresden were unwilling to stage the match without their presence. To make matters more complicated, Leeds fans had already started arriving in numbers ahead of the game and word had spread

Left: **Physio Harvey Sharman and assistant manager Gus Poyet take notes while the players recover from gruelling work-outs in the heat of Germany.**
Above: **In Dresden, fans board a bus organised by the club to take them to the game in the Czech Republic.**
Right: **The team itself were loaned the Dynamo Dresden team coach.**

LUFC
WHITE
HORSE
ARMLEY
CROSS GATES

bwin

LUFC
WHITE
HORSE
ARMLEY
CROSS GATES
OMRON
bwin
bwin.com
POLPUR
Gambrinus

Left: **Hundreds of Leeds fans made the unscheduled trip to watch the side play Czech side Slovan Liberec.** *Above:* **Matt Heath shields the ball – and his hastily customised shirt – from a Liberec attacker.**

around England before being communicated to anyone from the football club. "It seems we have a problem," said Gus, dryly while Dennis showed remarkable restraint discussing the matter with the Dresden delegation.

Back home, the late cancellation was met with the by now predictable "tour chaos" headlines. Some newspapers even suggested that the players had taken the decision not to play due to the fact that they haven't been paid. In fact the players had been paid for the month of May with funds provided by Leeds United 2007 Ltd under the terms of deferrals agreed when the club went into administration, and June's wages were due to be paid when the Football League took the decision to return the so-called "golden share". Nevertheless PFA chief Mick McGuire was misquoted as saying the cancellation was a blessing in disguise

The players in Germany were disgusted to learn of reports suggesting they had gone on strike. An impromptu squad meeting led to a joint-statement being issued on behalf of the players confirming they were "preparing for the season in a professional manner", but it was another sandstorm the club could do without.

All the while, Dennis Wise was busying himself with his contacts attempting to arrange a short-notice game. Given his emphasis on fitness and training, the postponement didn't unduly concern the manager, but he was more mindful of the fact that large numbers of Leeds fans had travelled in the hope of actually seeing a game.

Eventually he succeeded in arranging a friendly match against Czech outfit FC Slovan Liberec, only after the guarantee that they would field a full-strength side against Leeds. Liberec, a town high in the Czech mountains, was a two-hour trek across the border, but it was game on. The club also arranged for a coach to take fans from Dresden to Liberec for the game to ease the travelling worries of some of the many fans in the city.

On the eve of that Liberec game, Dennis, Gus and the entire travelling party descended on a local Pizzeria, much to the astonishment of the few locals who were eating. Leeds United took over the small restaurant for an enjoyable evening and, given the strong team spirit in evidence, even the most ardent of critics wouldn't have known this was a club that was supposedly on its knees.

Amazingly, over four hundred Leeds fans made the trip to Liberec and were welcomed with open arms by the locals. The journey was a nightmare for the fans and for one Gus Poyet who took exception to the care-free attitude of the team coach driver. "Watch the road you crazy man!," yelled Gus repeatedly, while the man at the wheel looked at everything but the road.

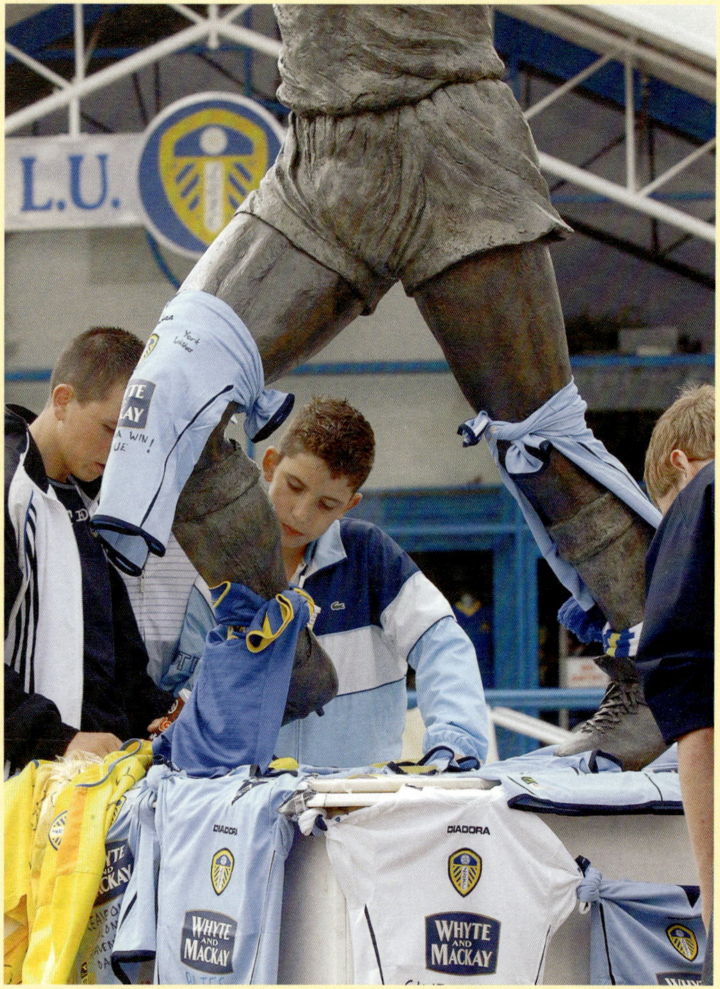

FLOWER POWER

While the squad were in Germany, feelings continued to run high back home and fans staged their own display of unity by laying flowers, shirts and other items of memorabilia at the foot of the Billy Bremner statue. Some protested about the board, some about the administrators and some about the Football League. Most simply wanted to show their feelings about the uncertainty surrounding the future.

TEMPERS HIGH

If feelings were running high in England, then it was only to be expected that temperatures should rise in Germany as United played the final game of the tour against Bundesliga side Energie Cottbus in Dessau. The game ended in a 2-1 defeat, but United had two men sent-off and at one stage threatened to walk off. Accusations flew about racial abuse from the referee, and it took almost an hour for the man in black to agree to speak to anyone from Leeds after the game. While Technical Director Gwyn Williams attempted to resolve the bad feeling, Dennis Wise took the players on an impromptu walkabout to thank some of the travelling fans. With the game's hostilities behind them it was clear that the strong bond among the players was getting stronger. Less than 24 hours later the squad were heading home, but only after a lengthy delay at Berlin airport while a Welsh choir and their group of musicians checked in their instruments.

BACK TO BLIGHTY

WHAT THE HELL IS GOING ON?

As the 'flower protest' at Elland Road gathered momentum ahead of the team's return from Germany, CEO Shaun Harvey moved to appease fans' frustrations by issuing a statement explaining the latest situation regarding the club's short-term future. It told that the constant requests and demands for information regarding the purchase of the old club by Leeds United 2007 Ltd were being met, but there were no firm indications from the Football League as to whether the situation was any closer to being resolved.

It was against this backdrop that teenager Danny Rose joined Tottenham Hotspur after 'resigning' from his position within the club's Academy, and media speculation began over the future of Richard Cresswell. The striker had missed the early pre-season games pending the birth of his third child, but he did take his place on the substitutes bench for a 2-1 defeat at Burnley. The fans again voiced their frustrations at Turf Moor and, afterwards, an emotionally charged Gus Poyet pleaded for calm in a TV interview.

The club's Open Day followed the Burnley game and over three thousand people visited Elland Road for the annual jamboree. The club's decision to hold a 'fun event' was lost on some given the ongoing climate, but the majority – who opted to believe that life must go on – enjoyed their day. There was a chink of light in the share situation, too, with the Football League publicly requesting a meeting with Shaun Harvey on the day of the friendly clash against Darlington.

Over three thousand fans and former manager Howard Wilkinson ***(top right)*** **were at Elland Road for the July Open Day.**

By then, the new season was just 11 days away and although Leeds United's name had been included in the fixture list, the club was still without the share allowing it to compete against Tranmere Rovers on August 9.

WHAT'S NORMAL?

Despite the public uncertainty and the apparent lack of encouragement from the Football League, the club continued to prepare for the new season. One important task was the launching of the new kit. A handful of players were assembled to pose in the new shirt on the artificial pitch at Thorp Arch, giving most fans their first glimpse of the new sponsor's logo. The man behind it was John Ross – a lifelong fan and chairman of the Safestyle Group – famous for its 'bog off' window commercials on TV in Yorkshire – who had pledged the sponsorship of his newest venture, RedKite Holdings, and their logo sat proudly on the new-look Admiral shirts. Jonathan Douglas was one of the players involved in the launch and, unusually for a player, expressed his delight at the style of the new shirt. The kit launch was followed by a routine 'head and shoulders' photo session for the rest of the squad who are called in at regular intervals. Many posed willingly, but one experienced player still waiting to sign his contract declined politely on the grounds that he had yet to sign on the dotted line. While the players enjoyed some welcome relief away from training, striker Richard Cresswell began talks with Stoke City about his move to the Britannia Stadium.

D-DAY

Friday August 3, 2007 will be remembered as one of the most important days in the history of the club. Shortly after 5.30pm – and sometime after a media leak suggesting a statement was about to be made regarding the club's Football League share – it was announced to the world that Leeds United 2007 Ltd had been granted the share required to take part in the Football League. But the decision came at a price. The share was transferred in 'exceptional circumstances' in the light of League rules stating that clubs emerging from administration must have a valid CVA. Following the Inland Revenue's challenge to the courts, Leeds United's agreed CVA was scrapped by the administrators, and so the League invoked an 'exceptional circumstances' sanction – meaning the club would start the season on minus-15 points. The club's immediate response was to appeal against the decision, although the League gave no indication of a time scale and there were just eight more days to go before the Tranmere game.

The announcement only served to further enhance the growing siege mentality within the United camp and less than 24 hours later, Jermaine Beckford scored his first ever goal for the club in a 2-1 friendly defeat at the hands of Wigan Athletic. Prior to the game, Dennis Wise grouped the players together in the Elland Road dressing room and came straight to the point. "We're all in this together," he said. "Hopefully something will change and it won't be minus-15, but it's something that's been put in front of us and we have to get over it. It also means we'll need 105 points to win this league now."

NEW FACES

After a summer spent watching the transfer market go by, the Football League's announcement was the green light to sign players. Ironically, the first signing of the summer wasn't a player who had been training with the club throughout the summer. With the majority of the squad on a day-off and others preparing for a friendly at Guiseley, goalkeeper Casper Ankergren answered the call to arms by jumping on a plane from Copenhagen to become the first completed signing. The transfer restraints had left the club without a fit contracted goalkeeper during pre-season and the void had been filled largely by trialists Scott Loach, a youngster from Watford, and recently released Chelsea youngster Nick Hamman. Ankergren went straight into the team at Guiseley the same evening and played the opening 45 minutes before his hectic day came to an end. It was a surreal evening at Guiseley with a normally nonchalant Dennis Wise surprised to hear his name being chanted by a handful of supporters as he crossed the pitch ahead of the game.

The 2-0 defeat suffered by what was mainly a reserve team proved to be the calm before the storm as, the following day, the club went into signing overdrive. The corridor outside the office of Alison Royston, the club's Head of Football Administration, resembled a doctor's waiting room as players waited patiently, filed in, and signed contracts before exiting again. Leon Constantine was the first, Curtis Weston second and central defender Matt Heath made it three before training began. After training, the rush continued. David Prutton and Rui Marques signed up before youngsters Tomi Ameobi, Scott Gardner, and Gavin Rothery all put pen to paper on new contracts with the club. That took the tally to 10 signings in just 24 hours, and there were still three full days remaining before the Tranmere game. Alan Thompson signed a couple of days later and young striker Tom Elliott, who had become the first schoolboy ever to play for the club in February 2007 when he made his debut at Norwich, signed his first professional contract. Tore Andre Flo also signed on the dotted line ahead of the new campaign as Wisey's squad suddenly started to take shape.

Left: **Youngsters Nathan Cartman and Rob Bayly in action in the reserves friendly against Guiseley.**
Above: **Seasoned pros Tore Andre Flo and Casper Ankergren were among the rush of players signing contracts.**

THEY'VE CUT MY BALLS OFF

Despite the apparent determination for secrecy, the 72 Football League chairmen were welcomed to the club's appeal hearing in London by the waiting media pack. Most rushed in without making comment, but one or two did stop to offer soundbites which would appear later in the day. Leeds were represented by Mr David Phillips and in a hearing that lasted 60 minutes, the Football League chairmen voted in support of the League board's decision to "punish" the club and over 50 voted in favour of a 15-point deduction. That sealed it.

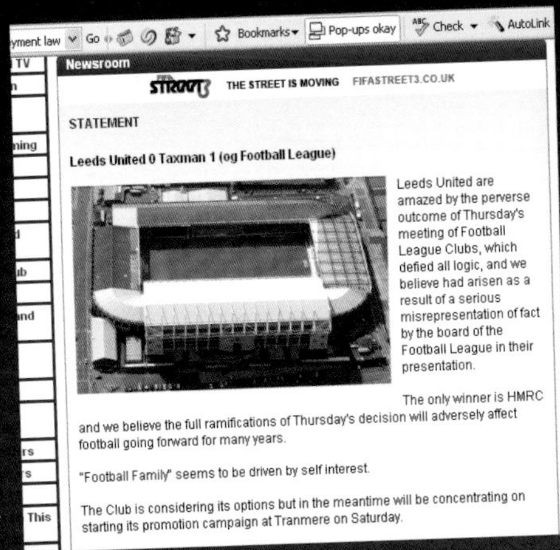

Newsroom

THE STREET IS MOVING FIFASTREET3.CO.UK

STATEMENT

Leeds United 0 Taxman 1 (og Football League)

Leeds United are amazed by the perverse outcome of Thursday's meeting of Football League Clubs, which defied all logic, and we believe had arisen as a result of a serious misrepresentation of fact by the board of the Football League in their presentation.

The only winner is HMRC and we believe the full ramifications of Thursday's decision will adversely affect football going forward for many years.

"Football Family" seems to be driven by self interest.

The Club is considering its options but in the meantime will be concentrating on starting its promotion campaign at Tranmere on Saturday.

A triumphant Lord Mawhinney emerged to tell Sky of his delight at the "overwhelming support received by the League board" – this was when the majority of the Leeds United staff learnt the decision had been upheld – while several chairmen, including Gillingham's Paul Scally and Peterborough's Barry Fry made it clear they had backed the League. In a London legal office near the SAS Radisson hotel, Ken Bates, Shaun Harvey and Mark Taylor drafted a short statement titled "Leeds United 0, Taxman 1 (Football League OG)". It was short, sweet and to the point. Some 200 miles north of London, Dennis Wise was stunned when he learnt of the news – some 30 minutes after it had been publicly announced. Wisey was heading to a Football League meeting of managers at Preston and promptly turned his car around and headed back to Thorp Arch.

It had been decided to convene a press conference for 5pm – irrespective of the outcome – and the manager was ready to face the media. As the press gathered in the medical room at Thorp Arch, Wisey paced the corridor outside. By his own admission, he was sick and tired of the negative press surrounding the club and was keen to make a point. One idea was to plaster the room in cuttings to emphasise his point about everyone being against the club, but instead he simply took a handful of examples in with him. Assistant manager Gus Poyet – often viewed as the calming influence – entered the room along with the manager, and there was a spiky opening to proceedings. Wisey turned on Phil Hay, the club's reporter for the *Yorkshire Evening Post*. "You see all this rubbish that's been in your paper?" he said brandishing cuttings from the paper. "It's rubbish and it's got to stop. It stops now. You're either with us or against us. What's it to be?" Wisey's stance was a curve ball to the waiting media who looked on stunned as Hay nodded in agreement and said, "I'm with you." "Good," continued Dennis. "Now let's get on with this."

Naturally, the first question was about the points deduction. "They've already cut off my arms and legs," came Wisey's now infamous reply. "Now they've cut off my balls as well." The packed room looked on and Dennis continued with a steely glare in his eyes as the questions poured forth in the hope of gaining a reaction. This was perhaps the moment that the United returned to Leeds. Dennis Wise, defiant and angry, couldn't have been more upbeat in the face of adversity and the coming together was apparent. Bizarrely, and unbeknown to the media throng, former Norwich City midfielder Andrew Hughes was sat less than 20 yards away from where Dennis was conducting his press conference, pen in hand, ready to sign a two-year contract with the club.

"Will the deduction affect your ability to attract players?" asked a journalist. The manager gestured towards the door and named Hughes. "I've just asked him. 'Does it bother you?' And he said, 'No, it makes me all the more determined.' I only want players who want to come here." It was an emotive end to an emotive time, but all attentions were now fixed on the weekend game at Tranmere.

THE SEASON BEGINS

12 MORE POINTS TO GO

It wasn't talked about publicly and wasn't even whispered at the club, but there was an unerring feeling that the opening game of the 2007/08 season was perhaps the most important of Leeds United's history. If victorious, it would ensure the season was off to the right start. If defeated? Who knows what would have happened and how things would have panned out...

In the event, over two thousand Leeds fans secured tickets for the away end at Tranmere with hundreds more gaining entry into other sections of the ground. Birkenhead was bathed in sunshine but, as with the title-winning game at Bournemouth 18 years earlier and the relegation match at Bolton in 2004, there was an underlying air of tension among the United fans. That mood wasn't eased during a first half in which Leeds looked like a bunch of strangers – although the noise from the away support was as loud as you will ever hear from any club's supporters. United-supporting Chris Greenacre put Tranmere ahead then celebrated in front of the travelling fans by making the 'Leeds salute'. The mood darkened, particularly in the away section where arguments developed among fans with differing opinions. The atmosphere was also tense in the dressing room where the players felt the full force of Dennis Wise's ire during the half-time break.

It was a different Leeds side which emerged after the break and after Matt Heath levelled matters, Tresor Kandol somehow bundled the ball home from close range in the final minute to make it 2-1. That was the cue for delirium

COYNE
1
STOCKDALE
2
TRFC

Matt Heath heads home then celebrates in front of the travelling Leeds fans as he scores the first Leeds goal of the season at Tranmere's Prenton Park.

STOCKDALE
7
WESTLAKE
11
BPBS

Tresor Kandol stoops to score – then somersaults to celebrate – as United secure all three points in the first game of the season at Tranmere.

24
24

Left: **Mutual admiration at Tranmere as delirious fans and victorious players salute each other.**

in the 'cow shed' end as the Leeds fans celebrated. There was even time for Jermaine Beckford to have a goal disallowed in stoppage time before the final whistle went. In a moment of euphoria, Wisey raced straight onto the pitch, pausing only to make a one-fingered gesture to the club's media manager, referring to a first win of the season. This was wrongly interpreted by some as a gesture at the Tranmere directors and in particular club chairman Lorraine Rogers. The incident was also mentioned later in the month when Wisey was rebuffed in his attempts to sign Steve Davis from the Merseyside club.

Once on the pitch, Wisey summoned his jubilant players and staff into a huddle and, with Gus Poyet belatedly arriving with a crash landing on top, the manager uttered words of praise for his men and reminded them that this was going to be the first of many. As the huddle ended, the players walked to the away end and more than one of them later spoke of the feeling of "coming together" between themselves and the fans as the travelling army celebrated the win with a chorus of "12 more points to go before we get to zero".

The atmosphere in the dressing room afterwards, though, was surprisingly flat. Maybe the emotion of the build-up had taken its toll, but the expected smiling faces, although jubilant with the win, were highly critical of the first half display and skipper Alan Thompson made the observation that "we had got out of jail". Tranmere manager Ronnie Moore later observed that he was disappointed with Wisey's reaction at the final whistle, but had the likeable Moore endured the same summer, he may have reacted in the same manner.

THE MACC LADS

The Carling Cup draw threw up a first ever trip to Macclesfield Town for the club just three days on from Tranmere and 1,250 Leeds fans headed for Moss Rose. It was the sort of story the media usually love, but a distinct lack of interest suggested even the most hardened cynics were all Leeds-d out. As it was, the players that grouped inside possibly the smallest dressing room they had ever seen included teenagers Tom Elliott, Fabian Delph and Scott Gardner. David Prutton and Ben Parker made their first starts for the club and a 1-0 win was secured when Ian Westlake scored 11 minutes from time. Eddie Lewis also made what transpired to be his final appearance for the club.

THE QUEUES ARE BACK!

Much had been made about the club's inability to accept credit cards for payments at either the ticket office or the shop. When the club entered into administration in May, credit card facilities were withdrawn and the eventual turnaround and subsequent approval of Leeds United 2007 Ltd as new owners ensured that the first home game of the season against Southend United was a cash-only affair. Despite repeated pleas from the club, many fans arrived with little time to spare before kick-off of the first home game of the season and the ticket office queues snaked around the West Stand car park as thousands of fans turned out to show their support. Naturally the Football League came in for some stick from the 24,000-plus crowd and all were in the ground for a rousing finale that saw three goals in the final four minutes, including a first from Rui Marques, secure a 4-1 win. The game saw Andrew Hughes make his debut at left-back in place of Eddie Lewis, set to join Derby County. Ever the professional, the USA international had put in a dogged effort during pre-season and despite seeing many of his former team-mates move on, Eddie had shown great resilience in his preparations. When Derby came knocking with the offer of Premier League football, there was no question of anyone standing in Eddie's way and the player departed with the best wishes of all at the club. As player transfers go it was a straightforward affair, and it was pleasing to see Eddie make his debut for the Rams the following weekend. Wolves defender Jamie Clapham had been earmarked as the potential replacement, but his loan move was delayed over the weekend of the Southend game.

Goals celebrations for Alan Thompson, Jermaine Beckford and Tore Andre Flo at the first home game of the season.

Above: **Before the Southend game, Andrew Hughes signs a ball for a young fan.**
Right: **Tore Andre Flo, Leeds' second goalscorer in the 4-1 win over Southend, speaks to LUTV.**
Opposite: **Inside the home dressing room after that memorable victory.**

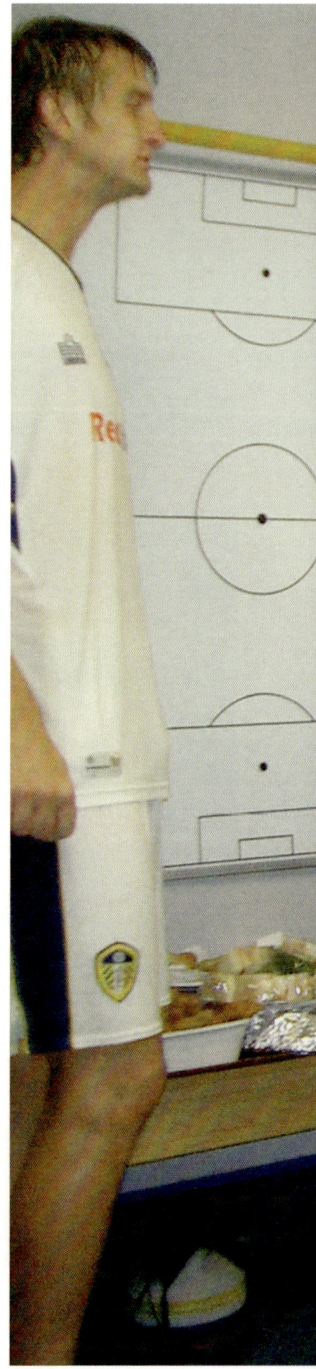

SOMERSAULTS, LATE WINNERS AND REWARDS

There were a few 'trademarks' developed during those opening weeks of the season. The end of game huddle perhaps gained the highest profile, but somersault celebrations by Tresor Kandol and late goals from any number of sources were just as conspicuous. At Nottingham Forest, Kandol performed his gymnastics early in the game before Jermaine Beckford struck the winner deep into stoppage time. After the game, the dressing room buzzed with talk of the Manager of the Month award. Gus Poyet was confident Dennis Wise was set to win the League One award at the first time of asking after picking up nine points from a possible nine. Wisey himself was outwardly non-plussed, but admitted a sense of satisfaction about the prospect of winning the award. That satisfaction turned to dismay, though, a few days later when after being confirmed as the award winner he had an unexpected visit at home from a PR agency complete with Sky TV crew in tow, brandishing the said award. Grudgingly, Dennis had one picture taken with the award and answered two quick questions for the camera. Unsurprisingly, when he faced the media to discuss the award the following day he politely told the Football League where they could stick the award.

Leeds United August 2008.

RedKite

A film crew from Sky TV's popular *Soccer AM* show arrived at Thorp Arch to film the players for its "Crossbar Challenge" slot. On the day the seniors performed less impressively than the Academy lads *(below)*.

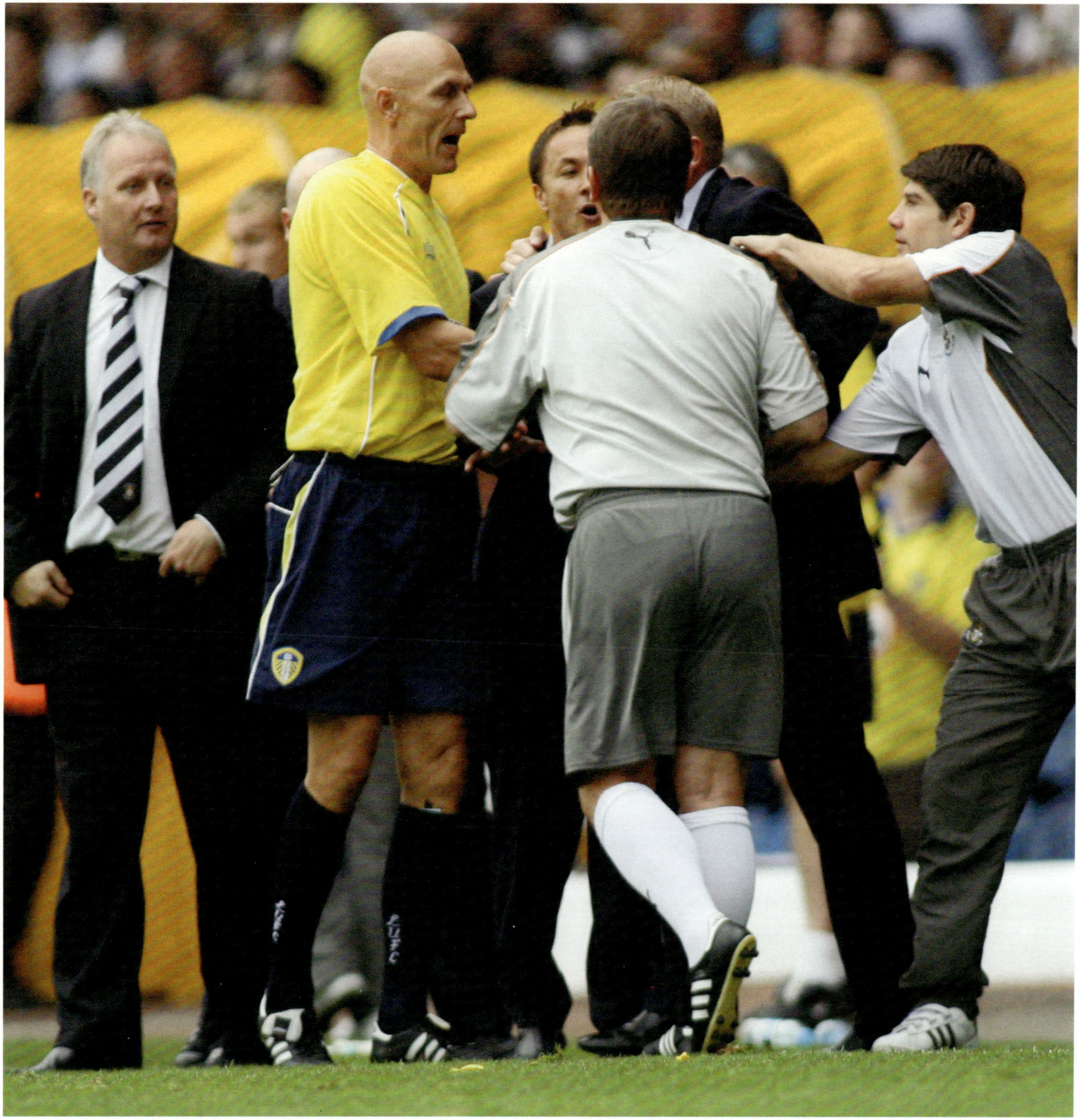

WE'RE AT ZERO, BABY!

ILL-FEELING

The media had billed the home clash with Luton Town in September as the return of Kevin Blackwell, but at Thorp Arch the build-up couldn't have been more low-key. With a much-changed team, Dennis Wise paid only lip service to the meeting with his predecessor insisting it was very much "just another game". In the event, it was a dour contest, a Tresor Kandol goal securing a fourth successive league win to reduce the points deficit to minus three. The real fireworks came after the final whistle when the two managers clashed on the touchline. Words were exchanged between Blackwell, his head coach John Carver – once his deputy at Leeds, too – and Wise before several other members of coaching staff became involved in a scuffle. The ill-feeling rumbled on into the tunnel and with Blackwell back in the Luton dressing room, Leeds skipper Alan Thompson played the role of peacemaker as the rowing continued between Carver and the Leeds coaches. Cleverly, Wise ducked out of his immediate appointment with the media at the post-match press conference and allowed his opposite number to play the incident down. It was only after Luton's departure and a conciliatory telephone call with Carver that Wisey left his office to face the media and speak about Blackwell.

"He said something about a phone call," said the Leeds boss. "I haven't got a clue what he was talking about. He has to move on. He's had his time here." Typically, Wise couldn't resist a jibe either. "It was probably the biggest game of his career," he said.

KANDOL
20
9

NO MORE POINTS TO GO...

Leeds reached zero points after the fifth game of the season, wiping out the deficit in the quickest possible time. The Hartlepool game was something of a day of celebration and with Jermaine Beckford scoring a stunning chip to seal the win it was a memorable day. Of more concern, at the very moment Jermaine was shaping up to lob the Hartlepool goalkeeper, club legend Norman Hunter was being taken ill on the press gantry. Thankfully he received immediate medical attention and was swiftly back in his role as matchday summariser for Yorkshire Radio. It was a radio station of a national nature that paid tribute to United's achievements the following Monday, though, when Chris Moyles broadcast a hilarious version of Enrique Iglesias's hit 'Hero' with the new words "Now we're on zero, baby." Within hours the song had been downloaded onto numerous mobile phones at Thorp Arch and was the ringtone of the week.

With 15 points in the bag, a club record start in the offing, and the atmosphere buzzing, one Sunday newspaper decided to pour cold water on the new-found spirit at the club by announcing yet another possible takeover. The name, this time, was former Newcastle United chairman Freddy Shepherd, a close friend of United chairman Ken Bates.

The truth of the matter was that Ken and his wife Suzannah had visited a nursery in the North East and had had dinner with Shepherd. Despite the club dismissing the story, it continued to rumble on until Shepherd spoke out at the end of the season and confirmed he had no interest in investing in Leeds United.

Norman Hunter in 1974 with his son and the first ever PFA Player Of The Year award.

0800 980 980 5
LSS
WASTE MANAGEMENT LTD
0113 282 4531
" the Big yellow skip people "
WASTE MANAGEMENT
TELEHOIST
Keep clear
SCANIA
YJ07 HSU

WAY TO GO...

Having clawed back 15 points from just five games to reach zero, the club celebrated in the best way possible. Nigel Woolford, whose company LSS sponsored the East Stand, arranged for a skip to arrive at Thorp Arch and a huge −15 was dumped into the back. The players found the publicity stunt highly amusing although Dennis Wise kept out of the picture. "It's their moment," he said.

KEEP ON WINNING

With the 15 points eradicated, the wins just kept on coming. A first ever trip to Bristol Rovers' Memorial Stadium resulted in a record crowd and another three valuable points. Injured summer signing Leon Constantine entertained his fellow squad mates with a rendition of 'Marching On Together' from the away end and goals from Jermaine Beckford and Tresor Kandol secured a 3-0 win, Jermaine's second of the night being a delightful overhead kick in the final minute. Swansea City were next up and the well fancied Welshmen were beaten thanks to goals from Beckford and David Prutton. The seventh win equalled the 34-year-old club record for the best start to a season and also accounted for the side who would go on to win the League One Championship.

Printed in the matchday programme – at the Chairman's insistence – the 'Real' League One table for the visit of Swansea showed United in pole position with 18 points. But the official version had Wisey's men second-from bottom with three. It was around this time that Ken Bates took another step towards recovering the 15 points deducted by sending a letter to the Football Association requesting their assistance in the club's dispute with the Football League, but the FA sidestepped the issue.

REFFING HELL

The build-up to the trip to Gillingham was nicely inflamed by Gills chairman Paul Scally telling the *Yorkshire Evening Post* that he had voted for the points-deduction because he believed the club's argument against it was "really poor". What undoubtedly was poor was the performance of referee Danny McDermid at the Priestfield Stadium and the subsequent shenanigans which surrounded the game. With the prospect of a club record eighth consecutive league win at the start of the season in the offing maybe the fact that the team had to borrow a set of socks from Gillingham should have been an omen, but no one could have predicted the drama that was to follow. It was apparent inside the opening 15 minutes that McDermid, a novice referee officiating Leeds United

for the first time, was keen to make his mark. Tresor Kandol saw yellow following a clash with Efe Sodje that left the Leeds striker holding his eye. Seb Carole scored soon after and all in the garden looked rosy but the ref seemed determined to stay centre-stage and after booking Andrew Hughes, there was a scare when he gave the midfielder a second stern lecture. Unable to resist, McDermid did reduce United to 10 men moments before half-time when Kandol picked up a second yellow card for sarcastically applauding a decision to give Leeds a free-kick. That dismissal stoked up an already furious Dennis Wise and words were exchanged with the referee as the two teams headed down the tunnel at half-time. According to the referee, Wise swore at him. According to Wisey – and a number of witnesses – the referee swore at the Leeds boss. Either way, it was a surprise when Dennis took a seat in the directors box at the start of the second half. "What are you doing here?," enquired the already seated club CEO Shaun Harvey. "He's sent me off," responded an unperturbed Wise.

Back on the pitch, United continued to look the better side, but the cards continued to be flourished. Jermaine Beckford was booked

Referee McDermid goes card crazy (left). Jermaine Beckford leaves the field (top) and later joins Leon Constantine and Tresor Kandol to watch from the away end in dismay (above). Wise's view, too, is soon from the stands next to Leeds United's chief executive Shaun Harvey (right).

for chipping the ball into the Gillingham net – despite protesting he hadn't heard the whistle – and moments later he was shown a red card, following an apparently fair challenge on Sean Clohessy. So Leeds were down to nine men – yet still on course for a club record.

A visibly furious Wise looked on from his seat in the stand, barking orders to Gus Poyet stood a few metres beneath him in the dug-out. Amazingly, the cards kept coming and Casper Ankergren was booked following an apparent conversation with David Prutton which the keeper was adamant the referee had misheard. Even with nine men United had chances, but by the time Beckford and Kandol had changed and taken up their positions in the corner of the away end alongside other team-mates and the increasingly irate Leeds supporters, the home side embarked on their only period of sustained pressure during the game. As the clock ticked down Wise watched helplessly as Ian Cox scored a 91st minute equaliser to deny United the win. The travelling fans were quick to salute the Leeds players as they left the pitch, but soon became aware that the referee remained in the centre circle – from where he would have to walk towards their left-hand corner to reach the Priestfield dressing rooms. In a surreal scene McDermid, surrounded by a number of security men, first walked, then broke into a desperate run, to the corner. Once under the stand he avoided the Leeds boss who was speaking to a number of stewards outside asking them for their names and addresses. Six of them freely volunteered and offered to stand as witnesses for Wisey, who knew he would face a charge following his own red card.

Before facing the media in the press conference, Wise took a stroll around the pitch to compose himself, acutely aware that he could face further

LEEDS

punishment if he spoke out of turn. In the event he let off only a minimal amount of steam. "He told me to f*** off," said the Leeds manager, remaining remarkably calm. "You can't do that, but I do have witnesses." (Those witnesses, the stewards, were contacted by the club and gave their full support but their words later counted for little when Wisey's appeal to the FA was dismissed as "unproven" and he was handed another fine.)

As the players grouped together after the game there was an air of dejection. "It was a draw that felt like a defeat," observed Ian Westlake. "But it was a crazy game to play in."

VII
Fire
exit

Admiral
Total waste solutions
RedKite

The 11th hour return of the 'golden share' in August meant that the traditional pre-season squad photo was delayed until September 24. The players engaged in much clowning and one of them produced an unlikely prop for Tresor Kandol.

15 POINTS? WHO GIVES A ****

GONE WEST

Two decades ago, Leeds and Oldham were habitual rivals. League and cup meetings were seasonal and a number of players made the short trek along the M62 to play at Boundary Park after departing Elland Road. When the two sides locked horns again in October 2007 it was ironic that John Sheridan, a 1980s legend at Leeds United, was in charge as Oldham looked to become the first team to dent the unbeaten start to the league season.

Frustratingly for Dennis Wise, he went into the game without his two main strikers due to suspension following the Gillingham game. He had spent Sunday evening and Monday morning desperately looking for loan replacements finding Mark De Vries and Wayne Andrews to fit the bill. They arrived on Monday afternoon so neither had had a full training session with their new team-

RedKite

mates when they were thrust into action on the Tuesday night. It turned out to be a largely dour contest, with the highlight of the 90 minutes being almost four thousand away fans bursting into a chorus of "15 points who gives a f***, we're Super Leeds we're going up". Ian Westlake remembers listening with much amusement on the substitutes bench before he stepped up to provide the *coup de grâce*. Just as it appeared like a second successive draw, Seb Carole whipped over a cross and Westlake arrived to score with his first touch. It was no ordinary goal. It was a volley with his wrong foot. In the 94th minute. And it was the final kick of the game. The away end erupted, and various bodies from the visiting dug-out spilled onto the pitch including an overwhelmed Gus Poyet. It was perhaps one of the most emotional moments of the entire season.

All through the historic season Leeds fans took photos of their travels following the team and sent them into the matchday programme. Here is just a small selection of those sent in after the game against Oldham Athletic.

HERE'S YEOVIL

As had been the norm for Leeds United fans since relegation from the Premiership, the release of the fixtures prompted a scan to check for new, uncharted waters. In recent years, we'd had Crewe and Colchester, and in 2007/08 there were a few more. Cheltenham was one notable new addition to the fixture list, but the most interesting was perhaps Yeovil Town. The former Southern League outfit were by now established in League One, but for Leeds United it represented a first ever meeting with the Somerset side.

The first meeting was given a little added spice following an internal competition at the club in which members of staff were asked to come up with a slogan for a T-shirt to mark our debut season in League One. The winning slogan, courtesy of our Head of Football Administration, was "Where's Yeovil?" Out of courtesy the club duly wrote to Yeovil informing them of the production of the said T-shirt and stressing that no offence was meant. In good spirit, Yeovil didn't take offence, but perhaps it was no surprise, less than an hour before the two sides met at Elland Road on October 6, to see someone from the visitors had hung one of said T-shirts in their dressing room. If it was meant as added motivation for the Glovers, it served its purpose with Yeovil performing terrifically well. The visitors appeared to be on course for a historic draw, but as the game entered the final minute, our Dutch loan striker Mark De Vries arrived to head home yet another late winner. It was a cruel blow for Yeovil, but another demonstration of belief from a Leeds side who continually fought until the very end.

HORSEPLAY

Never one to miss a trick, loyal fan and ardent supporter of the club Steve Parkin coined a little stunt with Ken Bates over dinner. Having just bought a racehorse, Steve was considering a name when he met up with the Leeds Chairman and the pair came up with the name "Minus 15". The horse was swiftly dispatched to Thorp Arch where its arrival caused plenty of interest among staff and players alike. The local media also took the opportunity to cover the visit and it seemed as though everyone was revelling in the spirit running through the club.

LEEDS
CLIPPER
LOGISTICS GROUP
Minus Fifteen

GETTING AWAY WITH IT

Goalkeeper Casper Ankergren was honest in his appraisal after Leyton Orient had what appeared to be a legitimate – and potentially match-deciding – goal disallowed during a 1-1 draw at Elland Road. The O's, the early pace-setters in League One, had taken the lead courtesy of Sean Thornton, only to see their goalscorer quickly red-carded following an apparent elbow on Seb Carole. A second-half penalty was missed – Tresor Kandol stepping up ahead of Dennis Wise's favoured penalty taker Jermaine Beckford – but a Carole equaliser looked like being enough to ensure honours ended even.

There was controversy, though, in the final moments when an Adam Boyd shot appeared to slip through the hands of Ankergren and over the goal-line. The keeper reacted quickly to smother the ball and the assistant referee waved play on. It seemed clear to everyone in the stands that it was a goal, but at pitchside it was impossible to tell, and the assistant referee gave Leeds the benefit of the doubt. "S*** happens," was how a reflective Casper later described the incident.

WITHDEAN WONDERS

Brighton's Withdean Stadium hadn't been the happiest of hunting grounds for Leeds in recent seasons. The makeshift venue, a tree-lined summer athletics facility incorporating one small stand, a pub, a crèche, and an adventure playground, is a one-off in terms of football stadia. Our 843 travelling fans were housed beyond the running track and were situated almost 50 yards from the nearest goal. To the left of the away section, was a cabin which housed the sizeable dressing rooms, and it was from there that the Leeds squad emerged blinking into the sunlight 90 minutes before kick-off.

Dennis Wise had politely described the Withdean as "horrible" and "a very difficult place to go" and the first half proved to every bit as horrible and difficult as expected. It was so bad that assistant manager Gus Poyet, often viewed as the 'good cop' in the partnership, took over proceedings in the dressing room and delivered 15 full minutes of home truths to a team he believed had seriously underperformed. Poyet's words had some effect, the team looked sharper in the second half, but it wasn't until a catalogue of errors from the Brighton defence gifted Tresor Kandol his sixth goal of the season that Leeds were on course for a first ever win at the Withdean. The 79th minute strike proved enough to stretch the unbeaten run to 12 games and lift United to ninth in the table, six points behind leaders Orient. On the back of the Brighton victory, Dennis Wise moved quickly to secure the services of Radostin Kishishev on loan, this time from Leicester City.

BRIGHTON PIER
L U
F C
LUFC

VINTAGE WHITES

Left: **The view on Brighton seafront was more impressive than that which greeted Leeds fans arriving at their temporary stand in the Withdean. They were so far away from the action that the closest they got to the players was when they ran out at the start of each half.**

I CAN FEEL IT COMING IN THE AIR

It's fair to say that as November started to loom large, Leeds United were looking a confident well-drilled outfit seemingly heading for a quite remarkable triumph. The favourites for relegation were now the favourites for promotion after overcoming the 15-point deficit, and the big question was: "Will anyone stop Leeds?" The off-field traumas had also eased and there was a sense of unity beginning to prevail around the club. But, nothing had ever been simple at Leeds United.

Down in London at Tottenham, Martin Jol's managerial future at White Hart Lane was in serious doubt, and on the eve of Thursday, October 25, he was sacked. Of more concern was the fact that Gus Poyet's name was immediately linked with Tottenham in a coaching capacity. Privately, Gus had already told Dennis that the opportunity to join Tottenham might arise. He had also explained that as he was working away from his family (who were still based in Kent) and it would mean a move to the Premier League with one of his former clubs, it would be an opportunity that appealed. Tottenham's official approach for Gus came in a letter sent to the general fax machine at the club – not by communication to the CEO or chairman – at 11.29pm on the Thursday evening. The fax was discovered by the Elland Road receptionist the following morning.

Once it had been passed to the correct department Gus was advised to stay away from training and his wife picked up his belongings from Thorp Arch. In addition to the bizarre manner of the approach it appeared that Gus had already been given the nod that a coaching post at Spurs was there for the taking if he wanted it. While later understanding his reasoning, Dennis was initially disappointed with the situation and his mood wasn't helped that morning when new loan signing Radostin Kishishev tore a hamstring during the final moments of training, prompting a hasty re-shuffle of his starting line-up for Saturday's game against Millwall.

In the evening, Dennis had a staff meeting, without Gus, and his assistant boss was asked to stay away from Saturday's game – with Alan Thompson taking over the role for one match only. Over a series of telephone calls it took until Sunday to agree a compensation package, after which Gus was granted official permission to speak with Tottenham regarding joining their coaching staff. Despite Wisey's disappointment, he wasn't going to let his assistant's decision to move on ruin a long-standing friendship even if it meant breaking up a management partnership in which each half complemented each other to perfection.

AGAINST THE 'WALL

While the "Poyet for Spurs" story gathered speed in the media – there was the small matter of an Elland Road clash with Millwall. For reasons dating back to the 1980s when football violence was rife, games between Leeds and Millwall always had an extra edge. As early as 8am on the day of the Elland Road match, Millwall fans travelling north from King's Cross station in London were greeted by sniffer dogs and metal detectors as a long day for the police began. In Leeds, rival fans were kept apart in the city centre, but when some Millwall supporters were taken to the stadium by bus, windows were smashed and there was a feeling of menace in the air from both sets of fans. The tense atmosphere certainly brought out the crowd, as over 30,000 turned out at Elland Road.

With Poyet's departure imminent and a highly-charged atmosphere in evidence at the ground, it went almost unnoticed that the visit of Millwall, the first club he had managed, marked Dennis Wise's first anniversary as manager of Leeds.

Behind the scenes chief executive Shaun Harvey lined up an unusual celebration for the manager. After approving the matchday programme cover he suggested a one-off spoof version be made especially for Dennis. Recalling that very few were thrilled by the news of Wise's appointment, but 12 months later his results had proved all the doubters wrong, the coverline "One year on" was changed to "Wanker to winner". Wise got the joke immediately, laughed out loud and pinned the artwork to his office door.

Mirroring the rollercoaster ride under his stewardship, the Millwall game was hugely entertaining. Goals by David Prutton, Jermaine Beckford and two by Jonathan Douglas meant Leeds were four goals up in an hour and cruising. Then the visitors pulled a couple of goals back and United spent the final 15 minutes protecting a 4-2 advantage. The Millwall supporters were kept behind for almost an hour after the game and it was suggested to the club afterwards that the traditional post-match anthem of Queen's 'Don't Stop Me Now' had provoked an angry response among many of them. Maybe the sound of Freddie Mercury topped off a disappointing day, but for Leeds it was 13 games unbeaten and the march continued.

NOVEMBER RAIN

HARRY'S GAME

With Gus Poyet's departure confirmed and the subsequent compensation package agreed with Spurs, Dennis Wise's most important job was to find a replacement for his right-hand man. The pair had a special relationship with Gus a respected confidante who often brought a calming influence to proceedings. To takc his place Wisey turned to one of his most trusted former mentors, Dave Bassett, who had managed him at Wimbledon and Leicester, and with whom he had worked briefly as a management team at Southampton.

News of Bassett's appointment appeared in the media before his arrival and there was scepticism among fans who labelled him a "long ball merchant". One of Bassett's first acts was to hold a press conference alongside Wise in which he reiterated who was manager and that he was here to "pass on advice when asked". Bassett

also joked that if United lost the game at Carlisle two days later – his first in the dug-out – it would be "his fault". On the eve of the Carlisle United game Wisey also drafted in John Gannon, a former player with Wimbledon connections, as first team coach. Gannon had been assistant manager at Mansfield Town, and had also played for Bassett at Sheffield United.

IT HAD TO END SOMEWHERE

The trip to Carlisle on the first Saturday in November marked the start of a mammoth week of travelling for Leeds United. It was north to Carlisle on the Saturday, south to Bournemouth on the Tuesday, and then west to Hereford for a FA Cup First Round tie the following Friday. For the team and most of the travelling fans the three games meant covering 1,200 miles in just six days and, having enjoyed a dream start to the season, few would ever have guessed how that one particular week was to alter the course of the season.

At Carlisle there was a buzz around the place. United had been given over three thousand tickets – including an area of a 'home' stand which actually overlooked the visitors terrace – and Brunton Park was set for its biggest crowd since 1976. Surprisingly, the 16,668 crowd failed to create an intimidating atmosphere and at half-time, after Jermaine Beckford scored an early goal, United were on course to make it 14 games unbeaten. In fact, Leeds were cruising up to the hour mark. Then it turned. Simon Hackney levelled with a wonder-strike and Carlisle woke up. The home fans found their voices and the players had the bit between their teeth. Joe Garner scored a second and moments before the final whistle Marc Bridge-Wilkinson made it 3-1. This was the moment everyone had been waiting for. The first defeat. Wisey's mood was no different to usual, although the disappointment was clear. "Someone was always going to beat us," he said. "We played well in the first half – I couldn't have a go at them for that, but whatever John Ward said to his players at half-time worked. It's how we react that counts, but we will."

Andrew Hughes described the dressing room atmosphere as "funereal" and he was right. The long faces said it all. One chuntered about being beaten by "The Dog And Gun". Harsh, maybe, but this was a game that had appeared to be all-but over at half-time, and Carlisle were among the leading pack.

Left: **With his new coaching pair of Dave Bassett and John Gannon** *(pictured)* **Dennis Wise tasted league defeat for the first time at Carlisle while a huge Brunton Park crowd including three thousand Leeds fans looked on.**

Leeds fans en route to Bournemouth (above and below). At the ground they saw a goal by Seb Carole (right) in a 3-1 win – and a heavy police presence.

BACK TO BOURNEMOUTH

Bonfire night was spent in the air for the Leeds United squad, on part two of the epic journey. An early evening flight from Leeds-Bradford Airport transported the players to Bournemouth in readiness for the game. Unsurprisingly it was another sell-out, and the media build-up centred around the club's last visit there 17 years ago. On that occasion, a hot Bank Holiday weekend when promotion was at stake, around five thousand Leeds fans stayed in Bournemouth over the weekend and some fought running battles with police. Windows were smashed and boats were burnt, and the south coast town had neither forgiven nor forgotten. The club had therefore asked for the game to be played on an evening, and a Tuesday evening in November was hoped to be a good enough deterrent to any potential trouble-makers.

As it turned out, the sleepy seaside town was invaded not by hordes of Leeds fans, but by scores of police as security was stepped up everywhere. Pubs were shut and locals scurried around casting nervous glances at anyone who looked remotely like a Leeds United supporter. In contrast, the officials at Dean Court couldn't have been more welcoming. With a club record crowd expected they seem delighted to be playing genial hosts. The kick-off was delayed for 15 minutes to allow for crowd congestion outside and, just four minutes in, Tresor Kandol scored his seventh goal of the season to give United the lead. Initially Leeds looked capable of racking up a cricket score, but once Bournemouth found their feet, they played a good passing game and Jem Karacan scored a great equaliser just before half-time. The second half was a different affair and goals from Seb Carole and Tresor Kandol answered those expecting Leeds to falter after their first defeat.

The final whistle saw the travelling fans kept behind while the home supporters dispersed. The 2,116 who made the long trip were in good humour, though, and had enjoyed their night. It would be around 4.30am when many of those fans climbed back into bed and it was 5am when the team bus finally crawled back into Thorp Arch. Just 36 hours later and the squad were heading off to Hereford. The tiredness was starting to show.

Hospitals
Germs Are
Closer Than
You Think!
Clean Your Hands!

ery Week!
OMINSTER
JOURNAL
NLEY JO
2 274251
sjsigns.co.uk

WAY OUT WEST

The FA Cup First Round threw up a first ever trip to Hereford for the club, but at the end of a week of lengthy journeys, the prospect of visiting a new ground didn't capture the imagination as it normally would.

The trip got off to a bad start for the squad when goalkeeping coach Andy Beasley was confronted by Sky TV cameras waiting to film the players on the bus. Dennis Wise was furious and demanded an apology from Sky. In Hereford, interest was high and a local breakfast show presenter, confirming the theory that there's nothing as stereotypical as someone who knows nothing about Yorkshire, upset local-based Leeds fans by playing the theme from the Hovis ads and cracking jokes about ferrets. For many fans, the journey to Hereford took the best part of six hours, although the main road into the town was a throwback to the 1980s with a Leeds coach parked outside every pub.

Wise had talked about the importance of the league campaign during the build-up and did tinker with his starting line-up. But after a week of travelling the team looked exactly as they were – knackered. The game finished goal-less and Hereford were delighted to secure a replay. After the game Wise was furious and deeply disappointed with the performance, but he didn't let his feelings show in an interview with Sky which was ultimately cut short due to fans outside the stadium asking for autographs through an open window. But his anger simmered, and when Hereford won the replay at Elland Road 1-0, Wise was perhaps as angry as in all his time with the club. Once again, he was furious with the performance and, possibly, embarrassed to go out at the First Round stage. It certainly dispelled any myths about him not being interested in the FA Cup. He was seething.

Left: **Goalkeeper Casper Ankergren made a number of fine saves to keep a clean sheet at Hereford, but was hurt in the process.**

ANOTHER ROUTE BLOCKED

In between the ties with Hereford United came a Johnstone's Paint Trophy tie with Bury. After beating Darlington in the Second Round, hopes were high of a possible trip to Wembley. Leon Constantine scored his first goal for the club, but Chris Casper's Bury side scored two goals from set-pieces and somehow held on to win 2-1.

It was possibly the most one-sided game of the season, but even the most ardent Leeds fan couldn't begrudge Bury's ecstatic celebrations. Perhaps of more concern to the supporters was a post-match interview in which Dave Bassett referred to Jermaine Beckford as "Darren Beckford", Jonny Howson, and "James" and Rui Marques as "Rio".

A slightly embarrassed Dennis Wise stepped in to spare Bassett's blushes explaining that his assistant, when his boss at Wimbledon, had called him "Dave" most of the time. Joe Allon, a member of the coaching staff, developed the joke by producing name stickers which the players wore in their next training session.

Above: **Wise with his joker Joe Allon.**
Left: **Striker Leon Constantine scored on his first start of the season against Bury.**
Right: **Jermaine Beckford struck twice to secure Leeds victory over Swindon Town.**

BACK TO IT

Having suffered a wobble, losing to two League Two sides in two cup competitions in the wake of a first league defeat of the season at Carlisle, United beat Swindon 2-1 at Elland Road to keep on the fringes of the Play-Off race. During the build-up to the game, Dennis Wise had lost his patience when a national newspaper journalist pressed him on whether he would leave Leeds if the offer of a better job arose. The said journalist wouldn't have known, but privately, Wise was finding the travelling difficult. With his family settled in London, he was making frequent trips up and down the M1 and, without the smiling, bouncing, Poyet at his side, that early-season glint in his eyes seemed to be fading. After the Swindon game, Wise was asked about United's chances of promotion – he had never publicly talked about the possibility of promotion. "That's a very naughty question," he responded to the local reporter.

ROOT IT OUT

With almost perfect timing, the Football Association announced in November that they were to embark on a "root and branch" investigation into the running of the organisation. Not prepared to miss a trick, the club's lawyer, Mark Taylor, wrote to the FA requesting a High Court hearing into the Football League's 15-point sanction.

The club had already written to the FA twice asking for an independent arbitration committee to look into the matter, but on both occasions the request was rejected with a letter from the director of corporate affairs Jonathan Hall. The second letter was merely confirmation that he thought his first decision was correct. At the FA's press conference to announce the "root and branch" initiative, committee member Barry Bright was pictured alongside Football League chairman Lord Mawhinney.

With the letter making its was through the postal system United made a first ever trip to Cheltenham and returned empty handed. Jermaine Beckford had a goal disallowed but after dominating the game, a mix-up at the back allowed Cheltenham's Steven Gillespie to chip Dave Lucas from distance and Whaddon Road erupted. A win would have lifted United to third, but even after defeat, Wisey's men remained in fifth spot. It was only a second defeat in 17 league games and the boss was clearly disappointed his players hadn't earned more rewards for their efforts. "If it hadn't have been for the 15 points people wouldn't be talking about us losing somewhere like this," he said after the game.

TICKET OFFICE
T: 01242 588117
CHELTENHAM
TOWN F.C.
NEXT HOME FIXTURE
LEEDS
SUN. 25th. K.O. 2. PM
www.cheltenhamtownfc.com
BENCE
FIXTURE BOARD SPONSOR
MITSUBISHI MOTORS
Cheltenham

SMP Portable Buildings
ECHO ECHO
VISITORS
Carlsberg
www.gloucestershire.gov.uk
JOHN WILKINS CARS
obsidian
BENCE

800 980 980 5
Carlsberg
Carlsberg
Admiral
Marching on together
ALL LEEDS ALL THE TIME
empiredirect.co.uk
CLIPPER

AT THE SUMMIT

VALIANT EFFORT

The early FA Cup exit meant a free Saturday so it wasn't until Port Vale arrived on the evening of Tuesday, December 4, that Dennis Wise's men got the opportunity to come back from that Cheltenham defeat. They did so with a comfortable 3-0 win on a cold and wet night at Elland Road, before a crowd of 20,036. Jermaine Beckford scored his 11th of the season and the ever-popular Tore Andre Flo came off the bench to score his second of the season. The win set things up nicely for the weekend visit of Huddersfield Town.

FOR BILLY...

The build-up to the first home league game against Huddersfield Town for 20 years had been fraught with sniping. Having applied, and been granted permission, for special dispensation to allocate Huddersfield 1,700 tickets for the fixture, rather than the stipulated 2,000 or 10 per cent of capacity, our visitors had been quick to air their disappointment. There was a suggestion that Huddersfield fans should/would boycott the game, but the fact of the matter is that just 48 hours before the game tickets were still remaining for Terriers fans. Dennis Wise further fuelled the fire during the build-up when he proffered the opinion that he "didn't care how many tickets Huddersfield had got" and "we should stick 'em in the corner out of the way". It was nothing personal to Huddersfield fans, Dennis had long been of the opinion that the away fans should be allocated the South East Corner – also known as the "cheese wedge"

– despite the financial benefits that a larger following would bring. Across West Yorkshire there were noises about the "size of the derby" and "the importance of the game". It was even suggested that Leeds were "playing it down". The truth is that very few considered the game any different to others – the visit of Millwall had pulled in over 30,000 and even the game against Leyton Orient had caught more imagination. When Frazer Richardson suggested that he considered derby matches to be games against Manchester United, the scene was well and truly set.

Sadly, with over 32,000 tickets sold and the biggest third tier crowd for almost 30 years guaranteed, events on the eve of the game provided a disappointing backdrop. The game marked the 10th anniversary of Billy Bremner's death and the club had made no secret of the fact that tributes

Huddersfield failed to make a contest of the supposedly "big local derby" game and the day belonged instead to celebrations of the memory of the late Billy Bremner.

would be paid. A special programme was produced and a minute's applause was planned. Unfortunately, the statue of the club's former captain was vandalised on the Friday evening with the letters HYC (for Huddersfield Young Casuals) daubed on it in blue. The said graffiti was being cleaned off at 8am, but word had got out and the local radio stations were carrying the story. There were fears of reprisals, but heavy rain, coupled with a noon kick-off, ensured the ill-feeling was confined to the stands and there was no crowd trouble to steal the headlines.

In the dressing room before the match, Dennis Wise took the opportunity to tell the players what had happened to the statue and the act of vandalism was fresh in their minds as the players prepared for the match. The game itself produced the biggest win of the season. Jonathan Douglas, skippering the side wearing the same number four shirt as Bremner, opened the scoring and Leeds went on to win 4-0 at a canter. Afterwards, both Douglas and Wise attacked the "mindless fans" for their pre-match vandalism, and the majority of Leeds fans departed happy that revenge was extracted on the pitch with a fitting tribute to the Elland Road legend.

Left: **At Walsall, Jonathan Douglas receives treatment for an injury that threatened to end his season.**
Right: **Alan Thompson celebrates a goal from his last minute free-kick that was deflected in by, and later credited to, Ian Westlake.**

WHOSE GOAL WAS IT ANYWAY?

With United closing in on a top-two place, a 1-1 draw at Walsall proved frustrating. On a freezing cold afternoon at the Bescot Stadium the highlight was the half-time rendition of "Champions of Europe" from over two thousand fans, many of them bare-chested and swinging their shirts around their heads in sub-zero temperatures. A Tommy Mooney goal looked like being enough to secure Walsall the win, but an Alan Thompson free-kick was deflected in by Ian Westlake in the final minute. The goal was the subject of plenty of conjecture – newspapers awarded it to Thompson – but when pressed, the skipper admitted Westlake had got the last touch, but questioned whether it made the difference.

The game, though, was more significant for an injury sustained by Jonathan Douglas in the final minute. Dougie was stretchered from the field after taking a seemingly innocuous tumble, and it was a major concern. At the whistle, instead of heading straight for the dressing room to celebrate the late equaliser, the entire squad, lead by Dennis Wise, headed straight into a room at the rear of a small gymnasium situated at the end of the Walsall tunnel. In there was Douglas lying on a treatment table and his visitors gathered around to enquire as to the injury. There were suggestions of knee ligament damage, but there was nothing conclusive until later the following week when it was confirmed that the midfielder could miss the remainder of the season.

A TIMELY REMINDER

One of the features of Christmas for Leeds United, other than the increased amount of football, are the annual visits to the local hospitals. The players traditionally split into two groups, one visiting the children's wards at St James's Hospital and the other visiting Leeds General Infirmary. It's always a sobering duty for the players, yet all admit to it being a rewarding experience. Andrew Hughes even took time out to ask if there was any more he could do personally to support the hospital wards.

Another staple at Christmas time is the annual carol concert and over 700 fans attend the free event at Elland Road. Not all players could attend but their festive message was delivered on a DVD along with the suggestion – from several players – that Santa actually comes from Greenland! David Prutton also performed a rendition of The Pogues/Kirsty MacColl's 'Fairytale Of New York'.

Back at Elland Road, a lack of positive assistance from the Football Association resulted in club lawyer Mark Taylor writing to request independent arbitration into the 15 points.

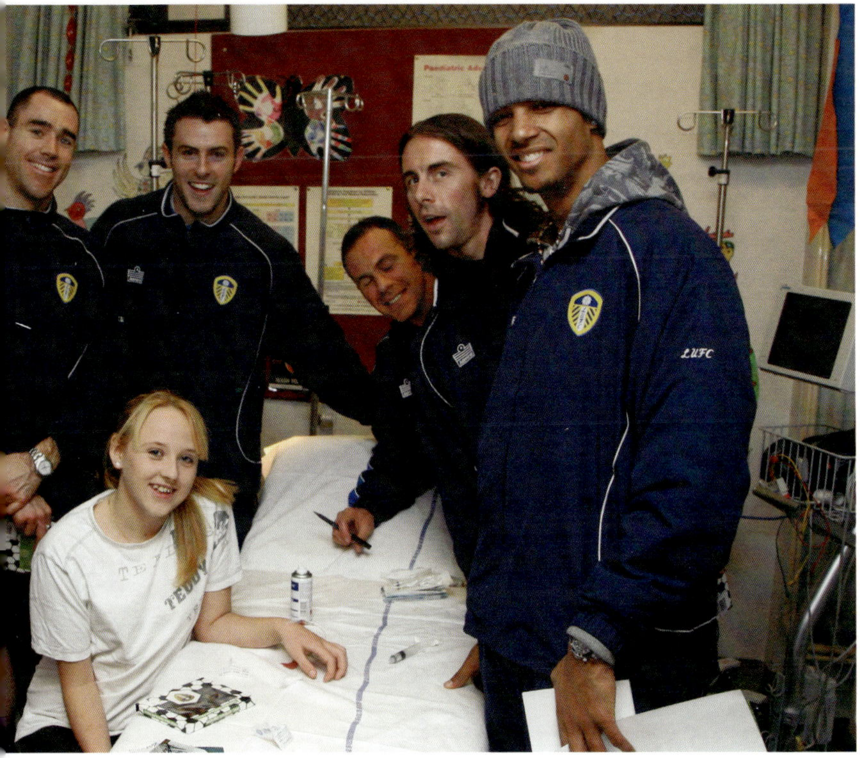

Above: **Casper and his daughter meet Father Christmas at the Elland Road carol concert.**

Top: **Christmas hi-jinks – photographed in September!**

Left: **The squad makes its traditional Christmas visits to the city's main hospitals of St James's and Leeds General Infirmary.**

MORE GOAL CONFUSION

Over 27,000 turned out for the pre-Christmas affair with Bristol Rovers at Elland Road, but the game was only memorable for yet more confusion surrounding the identity of United's match-winner. A Seb Carole shot took a deflection off Steve Elliott with six minutes to go, but with the man on the microphone clearly unsighted, the PA announced Jonny Howson as the scorer on the basis that he was closest to the action. Howson was duly credited with the goal by the media, the fans were confused, and it wasn't until after the match that Seb Carole confirmed his intentions to claim the goal. Then TV pictures showed a massive deflection off the Bristol Rovers defender, and the goalscorer was changed once again.

WE ARE TOP OF THE LEAGUE

Boxing Day 2007 marked a remarkable achievement when, after starting 15 points adrift of the entire pack, Leeds United hit top spot in League One. Jermaine Beckford's last-minute equaliser at Hartlepool – before he almost nicked a winner in stoppage time – proved enough to secure a point and, with then leaders Swansea City kicking off later in the day, the 1-1 draw at Victoria Park lifted Wisey's men to the top for a short while. The manager spoke of his delight while finding his way through the corridors to attend the post-match press conference and he challenged his players to repeat their 2007 form in 2008. The team coach was barely south of Middlesbrough before Swansea regained top spot, but with the top two sides set to meet the following weekend, all was set for a cracker.

Above: **Another Jermaine Beckford goal sent Leeds top of the table on Boxing Day at Hartlepool.**
Top: **As fans photographs continued to pour in, a boxer dog called Sox became a regular in the matchday programme.**

LONG WAY FROM HOME

A near 600-mile round trip isn't everyone's idea of a festive day out, but almost three thousand Leeds fans headed for the Liberty Stadium hoping to see the side reclaim top spot. For a few moments it looked likely after Jermaine Beckford scored an early opener, but Swansea were rampant and were 3-1 up by the break. Soon after the re-start Alan Thompson pulled a goal back with a free-kick, and rattled the bar moments later with another, but few inside the Liberty Stadium would dispute that the Swans were deserved winners.

The game was marred by an ugly challenge from Ferrie Bodde on Jonny Howson, and also by the young midfielder being booed as he was stretchered from the field. The Leeds players reacted angrily to the challenge and Bodde was sent-off, but not all seemed to agree. While delivering a pragmatic view of events at his post-match press conference, Wisey was challenged about the reaction of his players following Bodde's 'tackle' on Howson. "What do you expect?" he asked. "Do you not think it was a disgusting challenge? They were upset."

Below: **The Liberty Stadium was a fitting venue for the top-of-the table clash with Swansea City.**
Right: **After Alan Thompson scored direct from a free-kick, an ugly challenge on Jonny Howson provoked a red card for his assailant and an angry response from the Leeds players.**

The Welshman asking the question wouldn't let go, determined to provoke Wise into a reaction, but with the Leeds manager refusing to back down, and other pressmen giving weary looks to the interrogator, the journalist finally gave up and wandered off down the tunnel. There were more fireworks outside of the ground when a group of Swansea fans attempted to force their way onto the back door of the team coach. The senior players raced to the back to hold the fort before the bus was able to find a gap in the traffic and speed its way back to the M4. The year ended with Leeds United in third place in the League One table.

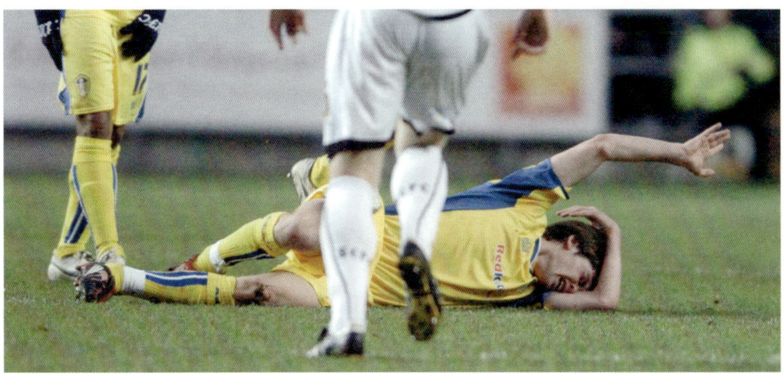

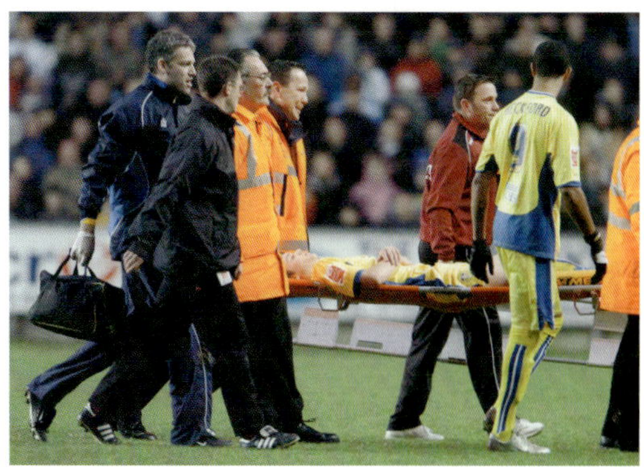

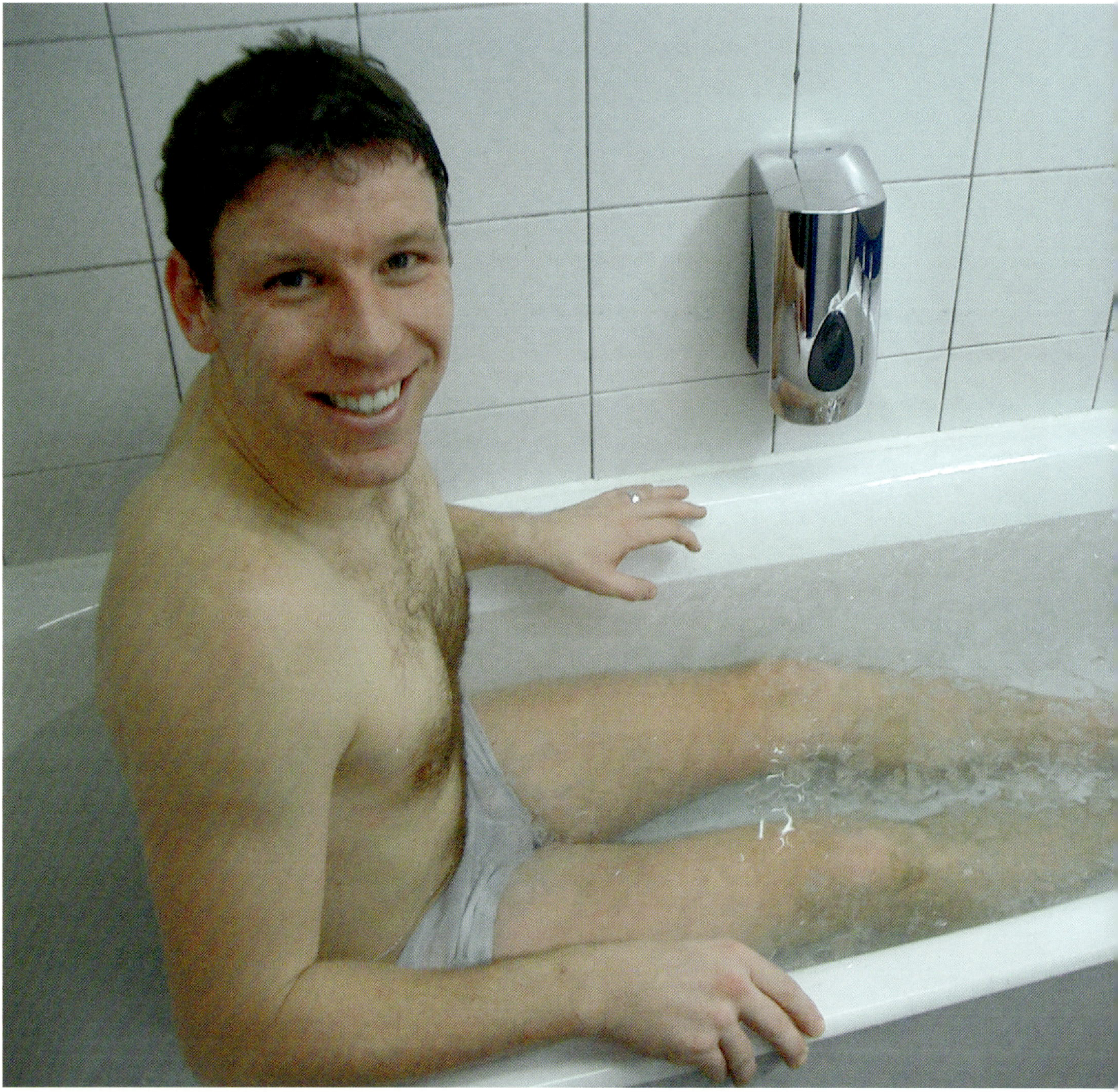

Alan Thompson puts on a brave face as the physios order him into an ice bath.

A wounded David Prutton signs a shirt for a young fan at the Members Christmas Party.

A BUMPY RIDE

(UN)HAPPY NEW YEAR!

As 2008 dawned, New Year cheer was in short supply for Dennis Wise, both publicly and privately.

Publicly, the year was ushered in with a spat with midfielder Shaun Derry. After returning from injury, Derry had been loaned out to his former club Crystal Palace where he was handed a regular starting role. But with a midfield injury crisis at Leeds, and no recall clause in place in the loan deal, Wisey simply asked Derry to return for the New Year's Day game against Oldham. Derry said he wanted to honour his commitment to Palace and the midfielder exercised his right to stay on in London. Wise was quick to voice his disappointment: "I asked him to come back and help and he didn't want to." Dave Bassett added: "It'll be interesting to see if he can trust that Neil Warnock will want to sign him permanently." Derry kept his own counsel before completing a permanent move to Palace before the end of the month.

Privately, Wise and his family were the victims of a stone-throwing attack while driving home from a New Year's Eve bash in Leeds. Dennis reacted by accosting one of his attackers and within days the story appeared in the *YEP*. Unsurprisingly, after the initial furore and "Wise attacks teenager" headlines, no charges were brought either way. Keen for a quiet life, Wise opted against taking the matter further.

It was against this backdrop that United kicked off 2008 with a heavy home defeat at the hands of Oldham. The visitors were 3-0 up before half-time

Left: **Dennis Wise vents his anger as Leeds are beaten by Oldham on New Year's Day.**
Above: **Tore Andre Flo is challenged by his soon-to-be Leeds team-mate Neil Kilkenny.**

and Oldham manager John Sheridan enjoyed a happy return to Elland Road. Although Leon Constantine scored his first league goal for the club, he broke his arm in the process, to seal a miserable afternoon for all concerned. The only highlight was watching Neil Kilkenny dictate proceedings for Oldham. Four days later he was making his Leeds debut against Northampton at Elland Road. Given the 24 hours he had, Wisey wasn't too keen on facing the media after the game. "I'll say something I regret," he stormed.

OFF WE GO AGAIN

There had been murmurings that the United bubble had burst since November, yet the team were still in fifth place and looking good bets for a Play-Off place at least. They underlined this fact when Northampton were beaten comfortably at Elland Road with Kilkenny making his debut and Frazer Richardson scoring the first in a 3-0 win. Rui Marques said an emotional farewell after the game before he headed off to join Angola for the African Cup of Nations tournament. Rui admitted it was an unexpected call-up, and one that would render him out of the Leeds side for a month at the very least. It would have been longer had it not been for some shrewd negotiating that ensured he could remain in England until January 5.

Peter Sweeney also arrived at the club on the day of the Northampton game. Chinese whispers had a tall, blond man in a suit meeting Wise before the game. Truth was a somewhat smaller dark-haired Londoner was meeting Wisey to talk terms about a move north.

Above: **Frazer Richardson opened the scoring against Northampton while Neil Kilkenny** *(right)* **made his debut.**
Far right: **New signings Peter Sweeney and Bradley Johnson.**

RedKite

RedKite

Above: **In addition to the stand behind the goal, Leeds fans also filled half of one side at Crewe's Gresty Road.**
Left: **Man of the moment Jermaine Beckford headed the only goal of the game.**

WOT SHIRT AM I WEARING BRUV?

With 13 goals to his name, Jermaine Beckford was always going to be the subject of media speculation when the transfer window opened. The boldest newspaper claim suggested a move to Premier League Derby County with the journalist who broke the story privately claiming to have picked up the tip from Rams boss Paul Jewell. Jewell subsequently dismissed his interest in the player, but not before Dennis Wise had used the link as an opportunity to remind the whole world of Leeds United's potential. "Where would you go? Leeds or Derby? I know where they are at the moment, but..." Not for the first time, Wisey was only airing his private views in public, but his comments caused a stir among Derby fans who argued theirs was a bigger club than Leeds.

The situation came to a head when Jewell was in the crowd for United's league game at Crewe. Sky TV cameras homed in on the Derby manager and with Beckford scoring United's winner the night was tailor-made for more speculation. In response Dennis, unusually, agreed to a live interview with the Sky studio after the game in which he reiterated his views about the relative size of the two clubs. Beckford, one of the more shy members of the squad, was also thrust into the spotlight when he was coerced into a live interview with Sky after the game. With cameras and lights pointing at him, Beckford struggled for words until he was asked about the speculation surrounding a move to Derby. "Wot shirt am I wearing bruv?" he asked a startled Greg Whelan in response to a question about where his future lay. The phrase inspired a legion of T-shirts.

THE FRIENDLY DERBY

The game against Doncaster Rovers in January was billed as "the friendly derby" match. With many Doncaster people following Leeds and little rivalry between the two clubs there was no great edge to proceedings. Sadly, there was so little edge to Leeds' performance that Rovers cruised to a 1-0 win to leave red faces all around at Elland Road and the manager lost for words.

Top: **Frazer Richardson wins a personal battle against two Doncaster Rovers opponents.**
Right: **Dennis Wise and John Gannon are frustrated in defeat.**

WE'VE GOT MORE POINTS THAN YOU

The trip to Luton was the start of a five-day stay in London for Dennis and his squad. With a match at Southend on the Tuesday night it was seen as an ideal opportunity to spend important time together. The build-up to the Luton game had seen a move for Dean Morgan collapse – despite the player's public claims that he was on his way to Leeds – and the match was billed as the battle of the clubs with point deductions. We'd got our 15, Luton had just lost 10 for entering administration. When Paul Huntington scored his first goal – upsetting the entire home support with his celebrations – another routine win looked on the cards. But with the game deep in stoppage time, Luton hit back and a late equaliser ensured honours ended even. Wise was shell-shocked after the game and gave an out of character press conference when he talked pragmatically about the result, only once raising his voice to describe "the poxy goal we gave away". Other things were afoot, and the world was about to find out.

Paul Huntington celebrates giving Leeds the lead at Luton Town – but it wasn't to last.

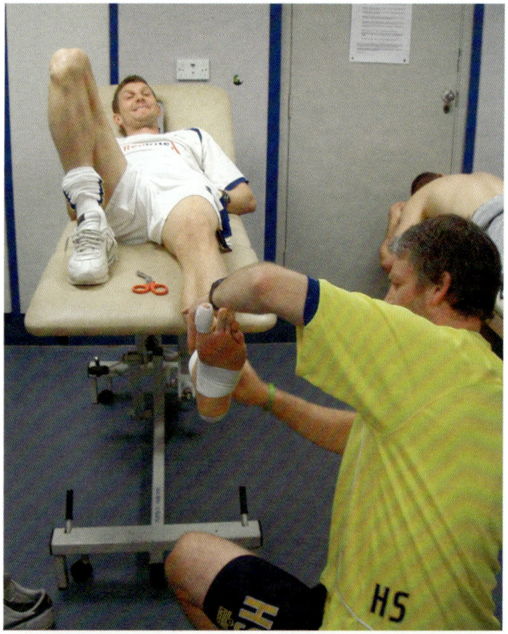
HS

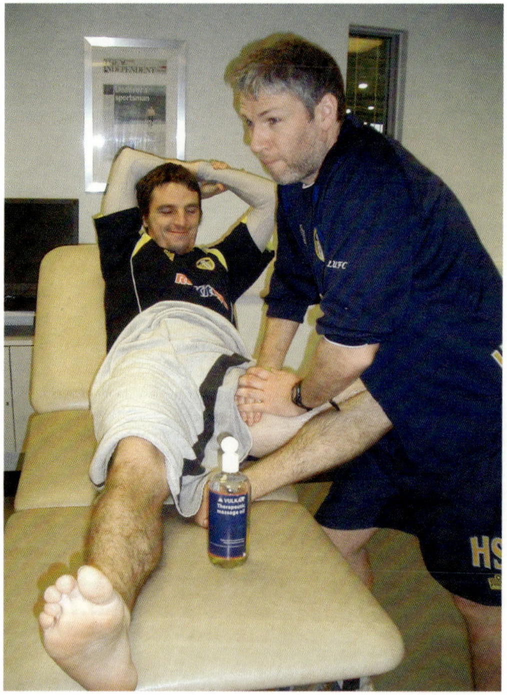
HS

HS

Above: **Superfan Gary Edwards was presented with a DAB radio before the Doncaster game to commemorate 40 years watching Leeds without missing a game.**
Left: **Behind the scenes physio Harvey Sharman works tirelessly to return players to peak fitness.**
Right: **Jermaine Beckford sported a short-lived Mohawk hairstyle for the game at Luton Town.**
Below: **Fans gather outside the unusual terraced street entrance to Luton's Kenilworth Road visitors end.**

TIME TO GO

The day before the Luton game, Newcastle United had made contact about the availability of Dennis Wise for a director of football post. They were asked to put their request for permission to speak to him in writing and, in the same letter, agree a compensation figure should they reach an agreement with him. It was very confidential at that stage yet while Dennis headed for home after the Kenilworth Road defeat, the players remained in the dark, wondering why things didn't feel exactly right. By the Sunday morning, it was clear that Dennis wanted to speak to Newcastle to learn more about the role they were offering. Unable to customise himself to travelling and spending time away from his family, it was clear that the Dennis Wise of January 2008 wasn't the same spiky little character of just a few months earlier, and the potential of a largely London-based job that would see him working nearer to his family had proved a big draw.

Inside Elland Road, talks swiftly took place about a potential replacement and Gary McAllister's name was top of the list. Technical Director Gwyn Williams made contact with McAllister on the Sunday

52 Sun Tuesday, January 29, 2008

Sun Sport
thesun.co.uk-sport

WENG WAR

By SHAUN CUSTIS

ARSENE WENGER has cranked up the mind games again with Alex Ferguson after they were paired in the FA Cup fifth round.

Arsenal boss Wenger (right) insists Manchester United could regret last week's money-spinning jaunt to Saudi Arabia.

And he said: "You switch off when you are away in a different country. So the focus could

Turn to Page 50

Tell Rom I'd come in handy!

THE Hand of God became the Hand of Cob as Diego Maradona paid a surprise visit to Chelsea's Cobham training ground.

Wood you believe it?

SPURS SIGN SICKNOTE II

TOTTENHAM beat Aston Villa last night when they finally landed centre-back Jonathan Woodgate — and he is already crocked!

Woodgate (above) has a hamstring problem that could keep him out for a fortnight.

And fans fear he could be another Darren Anderton, dubbed Sicknote during his Spurs days because of his injury woes. Tottenham have

Turn to Page 50

WISE UP KEV!

Keegan asks for £100m.. all he gets is Den to keep him in check

DEN DEAL . . . Wise is now in charge of Toon transfers

By STEVE BRENNER

KEVIN KEEGAN was lost for words over Dennis Wise's appointment as Newcastle director of football yesterday.

The bombshell came days after boss Keegan asked Toon owner Mike Ashley for £100million for new players.

Instead he has now got to work with Wise, who will quit as Leeds chief. Keegan will be in charge of the first team, while Wise will oversee transfers.

Keegan said: "I am reluctant to tell you all I know as I really do not know everything. I just do not know enough about it. So

Turn to Page 51

HAIR WORRIES ARE OUT!

Says cricket legend, Shane Warne

"I stopped worrying about my hair when I heeded the Warne-ing signs and saw Advanced Hair Studio. The Advanced Hair and Scalp Fitness Program (AHS-FP)™ includes Laser Therapy technology recently approved by the FDA. Alternatively patented STRAND-BY-STRAND® procedures can provide men with a guaranteed full and natural looking head of hair again."

Inventors of STRAND-by-STRAND® (patented) and AHS-FP™

Ring NOW for a FREE ADVANCED HAIR CHECK! or FREE brochure

0845 600 8899

ADVANCED Hair Studio

www.advancedhairstudio.com

Above: **Newspapers had fun speculating about the relationship between Newcastle United's manager and their new recruit.**
Left: **As the club changed managers Technical Director Gwyn Williams took charge of the team for one game at Southend United.**
Right: **Paul Huntington in action at Roots Hall.**

afternoon and by Sunday evening, CEO Shaun Harvey had also spoken with the club's former captain. A meeting was arranged for Monday evening with the plan being for Wise to take charge of the team for the final time at Southend on the Tuesday. An announcement would then be made on the Wednesday confirming his departure and announcing McAllister as his successor.

Like so many best laid plans, that changed late on Sunday evening when it became clear the story of Wise's departure was going to break in the morning's newspapers. Monday's *Newcastle Chronicle* and their legendary Newcastle United writer Alan Oliver were on the trail. Alan suggested Dennis had already resigned – at that stage he hadn't – and was having talks in Newcastle. That bit was quite correct. The problem facing the club was that, once Oliver had written the story everyone else would assume it was gospel and it would be repeated everywhere. Meanwhile the players and most of the staff, like the fans, remained in the dark. The club then confirmed that Newcastle had made an approach, but was still working privately towards the plan of switching managers on the Wednesday. Wise took charge of training and told the players to concentrate on Tuesday's game. It would be the last time he worked with them.

With speculation already mounting about who would be replacing Wise – his resignation had now been tendered – Shaun Harvey met Gary McAllister at his Midlands home, and the pair arranged to fly to Monaco the following morning to meet Ken Bates. A deal was agreed in principle, with McAllister keen to take up the role. Tuesday, January 29, saw the Scot on an EasyJet flight to Monaco while Gwyn Williams headed for the club's temporary training base at Tottenham's training ground. Both Dave Bassett and John Gannon were informed their services would no longer be required and Williams was installed as temporary manager. Goalkeeping coach Andy Beasley and football consultant Joe Allon stayed on to give moral support. Over in Monaco, Gary had agreed the formalities by 1pm and it was decided that he would take over as manager from the following day. Sky Sports were already claiming it was a done-deal, but the club was in no position to comment until the players could be told. And they were preparing for the evening match in a London hotel. The decision was made to make the announcement at 5pm, once the players learned the facts at their pre-match meeting ahead of the game. The news was greeted positively by the players, who were, by now, rather shell-shocked by events. That was reflected in the performance three hours later at Roots Hall as Southend eased to a 1-0 win. The new manager was in the air at the time of the game, but would be sat behind his new desk the following morning awaiting the players when they reported back in.

RETURN OF THE MAC

HE'S BACK AND IN BUSINESS

One of the decisions taken behind the scenes following the appointment of Gary McAllister was to keep things as low key as possible. The club had dodged headline after headline for different reasons during the past nine months and it was agreed that everything possible would be done to ensure McAllister's arrival as manager was as smooth as possible. There were no fanfares and no press conferences. On the new manager's first morning in the job he outlined his vision to the players, many of who had arrived back from Southend only hours earlier. The first training session, the following day, saw smiles on faces and a relaxed approach was in evidence leading up to the visit of Tranmere Rovers. Transfer deadline day – only McAllister's second at the helm – saw the arrival of Alan Sheehan from Leicester, Lubomir Michalik from Bolton, and an enthusiastic Anthony Elding who raced from Stockport County across a snowbound M62 to join the club. Being from a family of Leeds fans, striker Anthony was keen to have his photograph taken in his new shirt so he could send it on to his parents.

THE WRONG SCRIPT

Messages of good luck poured in for the new man in charge, but against Tranmere the "Return of the Mac" didn't quite go to script. United looked out of sorts and after conceding early in the second

RedKite

half, former Leeds striker Ian Moore made it 2-0.

It was a defeat which the new manager took in his stride. His first meeting with the media came after the game and he was quick to stress how pleased he was to be back, but at the same he was under no illusion as to the task in hand. "I'm here to help us get promoted," he said. "That's the brief."

Above: **At his first match in charge Gary McAllister has to watch his team beaten by Tranmere.**
Right: **Jermaine Beckford** *(top)* **and acting captain Andrew Hughes work hard to impress.**

RIGHT CLUB, WRONG RED

Immediately following Gary McAllister's arrival as manager, speculation started as to who would be his assistant. Sammy Lee was heavily touted in the media, but it was another former Liverpool player who slipped quietly through the Thorp Arch door to take up the post. After an unsuccessful [and probably unhappy] spell as Republic of Ireland manager, in which he was singled out for some merciless criticism, a refreshed and determined Steve Staunton emerged as McAllister's new assistant. With a wealth of experience and boasting a steely character, Leeds again had a management team capable of picking things up and re-igniting a season which on the brink of going cold. Two became three when Neil McDonald joined as head coach. The likeable Geordie, a former Carlisle United manager, left his post at Lincoln City to take up the role at Thorp Arch, and he, too, brought great experience to proceedings.

The new management team picked up their first point when Jonny Howson's first goal of the season proved enough to earn a 1-1 draw at Northampton on February 9 in front of another capacity crowd boosted by a sold-out away section.

Another sold-out away section saw Leeds draw 1-1 at Northampton with a goal by Jonny Howson.

RedKite
RedKite

Admiral
24
Admiral

A goal from the penalty spot by Jermaine Beckford secured Leeds a well-deserved point against Nottingham Forest.

CLUB IN PRESS CONFERENCE SHOCKER!

Negotiations had been going on for some time with various would-be kit suppliers for the 2008/09 season. Italian company Macron – suppliers to Swansea – were keen to break into the mainstream market and had put together a financial package in the hope of supplying the Leeds United kit. With the club able to boast the biggest shirt and leisurewear sales outside of the Premier League and being offered the potential to exclusively market and

sell the kit, bypassing mainstream stores, an agreement was reached in early February. It was decided that, in time-honoured fashion, the announcement of the deal would be made at a press conference, which was to be held on the Monday after the Northampton game, also the eve of a big League One fixture against Nottingham Forest at Elland Road. As a matter of courtesy, the club gave plenty of advance notice and informed the media on the Friday afternoon. There is nothing unusual in informing the media in advance, but the *YEP* ran a "club call mysterious press conference" story and Gary McAllister was even quizzed about it after the game at Northampton.

The upshot was that the rumour mill went into overdrive, mostly suggesting that the former Newcastle United chairman Freddy Shepherd was making some kind of takeover bid. Soon the Elland Road switchboard was jammed with callers anxious that the club was going to be sold and asking exactly what big announcement was about to be made. Come the actual press conference, members of the local media arrived and reported back to their news desks that "more mystery surrounds the press conference" – completely failing to notice the huge board in front of them advertising Macron. The guys from Macron were impressed with the attention and, with Gary McAllister and Ken Bates sitting side by side for the first time publicly, there was plenty to talk about after the sponsorship announcement. Twenty four hours later, when calm had been restored, a late Jermaine Beckford goal against Nottingham Forest secured a point in front of a crowd of almost 30,000.

ICE TO SEE YOU...

The re-match at Doncaster was being billed as the big game of the season. After the draw with Forest, much was being made about United's need for points and with Doncaster chasing promotion themselves, the game needed little hype. It was moved to a noon kick-off, there were suggestions of an alcohol exclusion zone around the ground, and the home club even had to plan a 'dry' champagne breakfast. Due to the early kick-off the Leeds team stayed in a nearby hotel, the same overnight venue chosen by referee Andre Marriner. On the morning of the match, Yorkshire was white with frost, but surprisingly, there had been no suggestion that the game would be off. At the team hotel, the match referee was spotted making an early morning dash to the ground, but there were still no major concerns at the Leeds end that the game could be called off. Blissfully unaware, the first notification anyone from Leeds United received was when the media team were overtaken on the M62 by the Doncaster chairman's PA who waved them down to indicate the match was off. This was less than three hours before kick-off, and there had been no official communication. Gary McAllister and his staff, becoming concerned, had also made an earlier than usual journey to the ground and they arrived just as Marriner was making his decision. With no underground heating and only half the pitch covered, it was clearly in no fit state, and the game was called off around 10am.

There was understandable anger in the first instance. McAllister was keen to play the game and gain points on a rival while the majority of Leeds fans were in transit. Many had even arrived from

far flung corners of England, including a group from the south west, while United fans from London were on the last 20 miles of their journey. That anger was replaced by disappointment and when Doncaster chairman John Ryan voiced his concerns about the handling of the whole matter by the company which managed the Keepmoat, it was clear that, in some quarters, Doncaster were also quite embarrassed about the whole situation.

By 12 noon, the Leeds squad were back on the training ground at Thorp Arch and by 3pm the coaching staff were spread across the country watching other League One games. By that time, of course, the Keepmoat Stadium pitch would have been playable...

SAME OLD, SAME OLD

Crewe picking up a point in United's next fixture the following weekend meant the team had played out three consecutive 1-1 draws. The team McAllister had inherited had therefore picked up only four points from a possible 21, were without a win since January 14, and had slipped to ninth in the table. The pressure was mounting but hope comes in strange guises, and after months of letter writing to the FA, the club went to the High Court about the 15-point sanction and was finally granted an independent arbitration hearing. Chairman Ken Bates demanded that the matter be aired in the public arena, but the Football League refused his request, and it was eventually agreed that the matter will be heard by an independent tribunal behind closed doors, with only the verdict made public. The matter would be now decided by a truly independent judge, creating hope, once again, that justice would be done. This is what the club had been hoping for since September, although without the cloak and dagger aspect of a private hearing.

THE IDES OF MARCH

GONE WEST!

The emotion and relief at the end of the Swindon Town game was almost tangible. After being at the helm for a month, March 1 brought a first win for new manager Gary McAllister and his reaction said it all. A Tresor Kandol goal secured the points on an afternoon that was almost overshadowed by events during the pre-match warm-up. Aston Villa youngster Stephen O'Halloran, a left-back, suffered knee ligament damage during the pre-match warm-up and was a late withdrawal from the team. Stephen watched the game on crutches and celebrated with his new team-mates before sadly returning to Villa just four days later to undergo treatment thereby becoming the subject of a pub trivia question: "Who appeared on a Leeds United team-sheet in the starting line-up, but never played a game for the club?"

United received a lively welcome in Wiltshire, none livelier than the one afforded to goalkeeper Casper Ankergren. Pelted with lighters and coins during the game, after the final whistle the big Dane returned one lighter to whence it came. He was duly reported, the police acted, and the goalkeeper later pleaded guilty to an FA charge, albeit with mitigating circumstances. One Leeds fan in the Swindon end was so angered by events that he wrote a full testimony to support Ankergren at the hearing and it may have been his comments which ensured the player escaped without a ban.

Substitute Alan Sheehan smiles as Tresor Kandol celebrates scoring at Swindon.

CALL NOW ON 087 12 12 12 12
lotto

Top: **Jermaine Beckford is the subject of close attention from a number of Swindon defenders.**
Above and right: **Once again Leeds fans fill the normal away end and overspill into another grandstand.**
Opposite: **Desperate to secure his first win as Leeds manager Gary McAllister goes through a range of emotions.**

THOMPSON
8
OHS

S.T.F.C.
SAFETY STEWARD
127

WELCOME BACK

When the chairman of the Football League clubs voted in favour of punishing the club following its exit from administration, there was a feeling around Elland Road that many had acted out of self-interest. Sadly, the season was barely past the halfway mark when Luton Town and Bournemouth both fell into administration and suffered 10-point deductions. It's doubtful whether either club voted against the punishment for Leeds and now, both faced potentially the same situation on their own exits from administration following failure of their respective CVAs (Luton were subsequently deducted 20 points during the summer of 2008).

To give added spice to the visit of the troubled south coast club, the appointed administrator was the former Leeds chairman Gerald Krasner. Krasner had been very high profile during United's administration the previous summer, offering his views, and now he had another vehicle to ride on at Bournemouth. On the eve of the game he visited Elland Road to discuss provisions for his personal arrangements. The conversation lasted barely five minutes during which he was informed where he would be sitting – not in the directors box as he wasn't a director of Bournemouth – and that there would be no security. On the day he kept a low profile and watched a very ambitious Bournemouth side lose 2-0. On footballing merits they deserved something from the game, but football can be cruel, as other clubs were finding out.

Above: **One time Leeds chairman Gerald Krasner cut a lonely figure at Elland Road when he returned as an administrator with AFC Bournemouth.**

GONE WITH THE FLO

In the days leading up to the Tuesday night game against Cheltenham Town, a decision had been reached at Thorp Arch that Tore Andre Flo was to retire from the game. The Norwegian had proved a popular figure during his short stay with the club and his goalscoring record as a substitute was terrific. But he had made just one start under Gary McAllister and, following a meeting with the manager, it was decided he would announce his retirement. In keeping with his good nature, Flo wanted to make the announcement only after informing his family and friends in Norway, and he issued a public statement late on the evening of the game against Cheltenham confirming his intention to step down.

Anthony Elding can't contain his delight at scoring his first goal for the club his family all support.

NOT AT THE RACES

Cheltenham Town completed the double over Leeds United on Tuesday, March 11, on a miserable night at Elland Road. Just over 20,000 watched – 565 in the away section foregoing the Cheltenham festival to make a first trip to Leeds – as the visitors took a 2-0 lead. Anthony Elding did pull back a late consolation, but it mattered little as the visitors celebrated. The Cheltenham game also marked the second appearance of loan striker Dougie Freedman as a substitute. It was the last time he was to occupy a place on the bench.

VALIANT EFFORT

The Potteries town of Burslem was awash with Leeds United fans for the trip to Port Vale in March. Over three and a half thousand Leeds fans had bought tickets for the game and, with a sizeable gypsy wedding taking place on the same afternoon a few hundred yards down the road, there was a large police presence at the game.

All-but relegated, Port Vale were playing without fear, but with Dougie Freedman in the starting line-up, scoring his first goal for the club, United were 2-0 up and cruising. Over half of the crowd was made up of Leeds fans, but there was a shock in store in the second half. Andrew Hughes was adjudged to have handled the ball – an incident which was replayed on a laptop many times over for Gary McAllister and Steve Staunton in the corridor outside of the Leeds dressing room immediately after the match. The video evidence confirmed the ball hit Hughes in the face, not hand, but a penalty had been given and Vale scored from it. Within minutes they were level but Freedman – the striker making his first start in Leeds colours – was on hand to score a third for Leeds four minutes from time. It looked like game over but, as Leeds had so often done to teams themselves during the season, Vale had the last laugh when they made it 3-3 with the last kick of the game.

That late equaliser saw an eruption in the main stand where three drunken Port Vale fans were forced into departing the ground after clashing with both

Above: **Loan signing scored his first goals at Port Vale in a topsy-turvy game that ended 3-3.**
Below: **Half those in the ground were Leeds fans.**

Leeds officials and the Yorkshire media. There was major disappointment afterwards and McAllister admitted that Leeds simply had to win against Walsall the following weekend to keep alive any hopes of reaching the Play-Offs.

There was still the arbitration hearing into the 15 points to come, but McAllister had already taken the decision to publicly distance himself from that. He was, simply, working with the tools he had. And that didn't include the possibility of being handed 15 additional league points.

Left: **training methods changed with the arrival of Gary McAllister but there was still plenty of importance attached to fitness work in the gym.**
Below: **Neil Kilkenny takes time out from the hard work at Thorp Arch.**

HAPPY (EASTER) BUNNIES

When the Sky cameras rolled in for a 5.20pm kick-off on Easter Saturday, many Elland Road fans voted with their feet. The season's first league crowd of below 20,000 watched United win a one-sided game against Walsall 2-0, while many took the opportunity to make loud jibes at the absent thousands. Jermaine Beckford scored twice and Leeds had won the "must-win" game.

Brighton were the visitors the following weekend for another important game. Having nosed their way into the Play-Offs, the Seagulls arrived on the back of a 0-0 draw at Nottingham Forest and claimed the same result at Leeds. As March came to an end, United were in eighth place, four points adrift of the Play-Offs, but with seven games still to play. Automatic promotion looked a distant dream, but the achievement of reaching the Play-Offs was dangling like a carrot.

OHS

ALMOST THERE...

NO APRIL FOOLS

As April Fool's Day dawned, one fan website ran a "Gary Mac Quits" story. It was all very humorous, except for the solitary bloke who emailed the club demanding to know if it was true. There were no fools that evening either as Gary McAllister's side beat Doncaster Rovers thanks to an Alan Sheehan free-kick. A gutsy, courageous performance was rewarded with a valuable win in front of a record crowd at the Keepmoat Stadium. The travelling fans sang "We've filled your ground for you" and Doncaster goalkeeper Neil Sullivan was spotted smiling in response to chants of "Sully is a Leeds fan".

D-DAY APPROACHES

As the final lap of the season dawned, all talk still surrounded the arbitration hearing regarding the 15 points. The club had received confirmation that the hearing would start on Wednesday, April 15, and was expected to last for three days. Unsurprisingly, the club was inundated with calls as to when any announcement could be expected, but neither Leeds United nor the Football League were in a position to be certain about the date or the outcome.

O, O, O, IT'S MAGIC

A first trip to Leyton Orient for over 40 years produced what Gary McAllister described as one of the best team performances since his arrival. Paul Huntington and Jermaine Beckford scored the goals to secure a 2-0 win and the bandwagon seemed firmly on the move again. Mysteriously, Bradley Johnson, who delivered the cross, was credited with the first goal in some quarters and, in a twist of irony, one fan threatened his local bookmaker with arbitration after an initial refusal to pay-up on the correct scorer! O's manager Martin Ling had also been on the wrong end of some stick from the travelling fans after comments attributed to him appeared in several newspapers regarding the points deduction.

Right: **Leeds fans packed into the old East Stand at Orient's Brisbane Road are delighted to see Paul Huntington give Leeds the lead then race towards them to celebrate.**

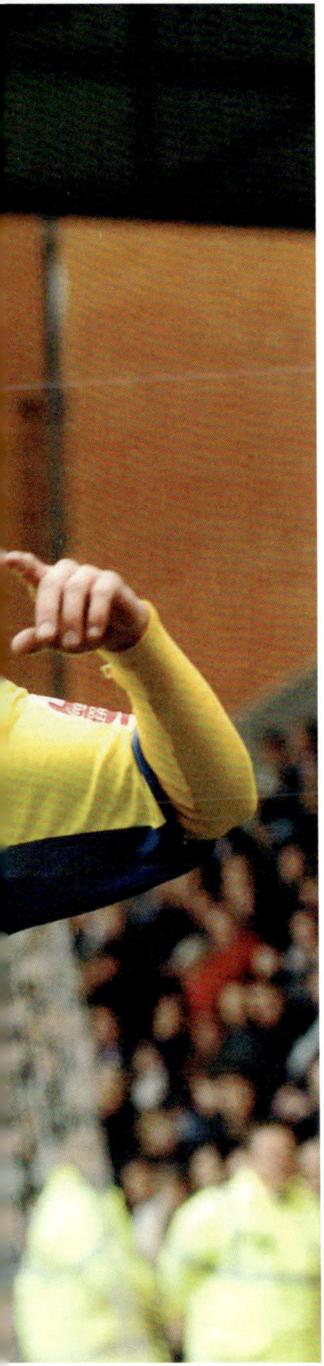

Saper Glass INDUSTRIES LTD

OH, DOUGIE, DOUGIE

Despite widespread acclaim for loan striker Dougie Freedman, his impact was still being underestimated. While many appreciated his efforts on the pitch, few saw the time he spent on the training ground talking with and encouraging the club's young strikers. Having a family in London, Freedman was allowed to balance his time between a northern hotel and the family home, but he was never less than 100 per cent committed to the cause. His private desire was to drive Leeds into the Championship and when he scored twice to complete a marvellous second-half comeback against Carlisle at Elland Road that dream looked to be on course. Jonny Howson was the other goalscorer in a 3-2 win against the second-placed side. Leeds were now four points clear of seventh-placed Walsall and a place in the Play-Offs was all-but secure.

Sadly, the clash with the Cumbrians was to leave the Carlisle-born Paul Huntington with a headache. His zealous celebrating – in front of the away fans – prompted an angry response from the Carlisle players and supporters. The following day threats were made by phone to Huntington's family and by Monday the training ground, too, was receiving threatening phonecalls. Huntington, a quiet and unassuming character, contacted the *Carlisle News And Star* newspaper to apologise publicly for any offence he caused.

Two goals by Dougie Freedman saw Leeds beat Carlisle and move ever closer to a place in the Play-Offs.

PLENTY TO SAY

The speculation surrounding the arbitration hearing prompted opinions galore from the club's League One rivals. Swansea manager Roberto Martinez proffered the opinion that Leeds had "bent" the rules while Doncaster chairman John Ryan said: "Would Bournemouth, Luton, Rotherham – all the other teams that have lost 10 points, take on the Football League? I think it's a nonsense." Even Carlisle manager John Ward made comments – taken out of context – and he quickly moved to re-dress the balance by stating in a national radio interview that he could see exactly why Leeds United had fought for a hearing and even offered sympathy as to the club's plight. Chairman Ken Bates was monitoring the press coverage closely, particularly anything that inferred the club had done wrong. By the end of the season, the club's Academy had profited to the tune of £11,000 in legal settlements from various media outlets. Apologies were also printed in several newspapers.

RedKite

RedKite

SIDESHOW

The first derby match at Huddersfield for 20 years was largely overshadowed by speculation surrounding the arbitration hearing in London. With the hearing due to commence the morning after, and Walsall failing to pick up maximum points against Bristol Rovers, the 1-0 defeat was barely noted as it did little to change the league table. Instead all thoughts were on the possible outcomes of the points hearing.

It was only clear that if the club was handed back the 15 points before the weekend, a win in the next game at Millwall could guarantee automatic promotion. There were guesses, conspiracy theories and much speculation – but the truth of the matter was that no one had any idea what the outcome of the hearing would be. In keeping with the confidentiality surrounding the matter, the club had not announced where the hearing would be held, but Sky TV were still present to greet Ken Bates when he arrived. "Have you nothing better to do?" he enquired as he breezed into the venue.

Back in Leeds there was plenty of talk but Gary McAllister, having never suffered the loss of the points, was able to say honestly that he wasn't banking on anything being returned and his priority was to ensure a top-six finish, with or without the 15 points. Actually, among the players at Thorp Arch, there was more talk about the weekend game at Millwall. As a Crystal Palace employee, Dougie Freedman had a few stories to share, and Leon Constantine jokingly did little for the confidence of some when he regaled a tale about a pitch invader during his time at the Den. At the end of the second day of arbitration the first "leak" came in the form of a radio announcement that the hearing would go into a fourth day with an announcement to be made on May 19. The first part was correct, but the second – wildly inaccurate – caused pandemonium among League One clubs as the date fell after the end of the League One fixtures and in the middle of the Play-Offs schedule. Leeds responded by bringing the story to the attention of the panel on the Friday morning and an announcement soon followed confirming that a decision would be made by Thursday May 1, 48 hours before all clubs played the final game. That still left the unique situation where, should Leeds receive the 15 points back, the club could be automatically promoted without knowing it. In the real world, McAllister and his players knew a win at Millwall would all-but secure a Play-Off spot.

Left: **The game away to Huddersfield produced Leeds' first defeat in seven games – as well as plenty of photographic opportunities for fans (and Sox!) at the Galpharm Stadium.**

E-I E-I E-I-O

Under normal circumstances, promotion back to the Championship would have been won at Millwall on what should have been a historic day for the club. Goals from David Prutton and Andrew Hughes (his first for the club, prompting an exuberant celebration) secured a 2-0 win and the result confirmed that Leeds United would end the season with the second-best playing record in League One. That fact, too, will probably inspire another pub quiz question...

The Metropolitan Police mounted their most costly ever football operation – there were over 400 officers on duty – and although the atmosphere was hostile, the day passed off without incident. Gary McAllister wasn't particularly happy with the performance, but publicly he reminded the media that over the season his players hadn't had the credit they deserved. "We haven't had any away from Elland Road," he pointed out. The following Monday, the hearing came to a close and everyone awaited the announcement with baited breath.

The atmosphere in the stands was tense during Leeds' visit to the Den.

K & T HEATING SERVICES LTD
Coca-Cola
Coca-Cola
RedKite
JOHNSON
16
OHS
14
22
37
OHS
2

MISSION ACCOMPLISHED

A balmy April evening at the picturesquc setting of Yeovil Town's Huish Park proved the backdrop for Leeds United to secure a place in the Play-Offs. The game had been moved to a Friday evening, but it didn't deter thousands of Leeds fans from travelling. The visitors were scattered in all areas of the ground and were quick to make themselves heard when Dougie Freedman scored what proved to be the only goal of the game in the fourth minute. The only blot was the second-half sending off of Alan Sheehan, leading to a suspension which was to cost him his place in the team for the Play-Off semi-finals.

Above: **The majority of Leeds fans at Huish Park were on the open terracing behind one goal but there were hundreds more spread all round the ground enjoying the evening as Dougie Freedman** ***(right)*** **scored the goal that secured a Play-Off slot.**

CHEERS TO YOU

The annual Player of the Year dinner at the end of April saw Jermaine Beckford pick up a bumper crop of the awards. Not only did he win Player of the Year and Players' Player of the Year, but he also collected the Goal of the Season. Jonny Howson took all the Young Player awards and Andrew Hughes – one of the real characters in the squad – collected the chairman's Special Award for his contribution on and off the field.

IT ALL ENDS IN TEARS

NIL POINTS

May 1 was the day Leeds United, all the other League One clubs and the Football League itself had waited for. The announcement of the decision of the independent three-man arbitration panel, chaired by Sir Phillip Otton, on the points deduction. The panel's decision was made public at 5pm and confirmed that no points would be re-instated. No one at the club had any inkling as to the outcome until communication was received from the panel some 30 minutes before the public announcement. One group of fans gathered at Elland Road hoping to celebrate, saw their optimism deflated, and within the club there was an initial feeling of disappointment that justice hadn't been done. Chairman Ken Bates reacted by saying the club had lost on "a technicality", but both Leeds United and the Football League said that was now the end of the matter. After nine months fighting the various authorities for a fair hearing, the arbitration ruling had been made and while the club was not fully supportive of the league's decision, the ruling was confirmed, and it drew a line under the whole affair. It was time to move on.

GREATEST FANS THE WORLD HAS EVER SEEN

One of the features of the bleak mid-winter had been the launch of an online challenge to uncover a fan in every country in the world. Over eight thousand fans from around the globe registered their details. There was the prize of an all-expenses paid VIP trip to Elland Road promised to one lucky fan, and

a guest, drawn from the list at random after the registration period ended. So it was that Leisa and Steve Simpson travelled from Coffs Harbour, Australia, and were astonished to arrive at Leeds Bradford Airport to find a waiting media throng. Preceding the couple through the arrival gates at LBA a slightly astonished BBC presenter Michaela Strachan wondered if the reception committee was for her, before realising the media interest was in two tired but smiling travellers from Down Under.

On arrival, the very first words from a concerned Steve were "Did we get our points back?" "Sadly not Steve," responded Ken Bates. "But we're in the Play-Offs and we're going to make sure you have a bloody good time while you are here." Their trip saw the couple meet fellow countryman Neil Kilkenny, attend the Annual Members Club Dinner, and be special guests at the final League One game of the season at home to Gillingham.

Definitions and therefore figures vary, but all totals put the number of countries around the globe at over 200. There were just 28 countries – most of them tiny or island states – from which the club hadn't heard when the challenge came to an end. Fans were uncovered in Mozambique, the Cayman Islands and even Mongolia, and henceforth the aim is to improve communication between the club and its overseas fanbase.

Above: **Greatest Fans prize winners Leisa and Steve Simpson met Ken Bates and** *(below)* **Australian international Neil Kilkenny.**

POETIC JUSTICE

The curtain came down on the league season in front of a full-house. With the upper tier of the East Stand open for the first time for a football match in two years, Elland Road's season-best 38,256 watched two second-half goals relegate Gillingham from League One. United chairman Ken Bates, who had provided free programmes for all who attended, had said it would be "poetic justice" if the Gills were to fall at Elland Road. Bates had not forgotten the comments made by Gillingham chairman Paul Scally back in August and September, and his wish was granted. An unhappy Scally accused the Leeds chairman of whipping up an atmosphere against him in the ground, but the crowd – also the biggest at any Football League game of the season – needed no incentive. They, too, remembered what Scally had said and welcomed the opportunity to remind him. The final day results – Doncaster losing at Cheltenham – ensured a Play-Off semi-final meeting with Carlisle.

Top: **Scott Gardner in action – plus David Prutton, Tresor Kandol and Andrew Hughes celebrating the second goal – against Gillingham.**
Left: **Bradley Johnson consoles a relegated Gills player, before he and the squad salute the Leeds fans.**

RedKite
9

15

DOUGIE'S LATE SHOW

Even before the opponents were known, the club had sold tickets for the home leg of the Play-Off semi-final. In the event it was decided that Leeds would play on Monday, May 12, with the second leg taking place at Carlisle just three nights later. Unsurprisingly, demand from Leeds fans saw most of Elland Road sold-out in a matter of days – although Carlisle failed to sell their 1,700 allocation for the South East Corner.

In the build-up there was a suggestion of over-confidence from the Leeds camp, but such a claim was far removed from the truth. There was a quiet confidence, but equally there was an air of trepidation. Outside of Thorp Arch, though, there was expectancy that a Wembley appearance was a formality – and that expectation became known to the squad who knew that Leeds fans, if not the whole footballing world, expected them to progress.

Perhaps because of this a certain edginess was apparent once the game kicked off and Carlisle were leading 2-0 as the game entered stoppage time. United's season was on the verge of all-but ending in front of a huge crowd on home soil, but Dougie Freedman snatched a lifeline in the 96th minute when he pulled a goal back. Suddenly, the emotional pendulum had swung again, and it was Leeds who would head to Carlisle rejuvenated. After that goal, confidence in the camp was genuinely high.

Opposite: **Jermaine Beckford, Jonathan Douglas and Jonny Howson battle hard to please the crowd and break down Carlisle in the Play-Off semi-final first leg.**
Left: **With the team trailing 2-0 Dougie Freedman scored in the final minute to give hope and confidence for the second leg.**

Admiral
SPORTSWEAR

WEMBLEY HERE WE COME

The atmosphere at Brunton Park for the second leg was akin to that of any of the big do-or-die games in recent years. Bournemouth in 1990, Sheffield United in 1992, Bolton in 2004 and Preston in 2006. It was all to play for and the atmosphere could be cut with a knife. Despite taking over three thousand fans to the league fixture in November, United were allocated just 2,000 tickets for the Play-Off semi-final and those crammed onto the tiny away terrace looked at the vast open spaces in the Carlisle areas wishing their mates were there. What followed was up there with the great Leeds United nights of all time.

Jonny Howson levelled the aggregate scores and, typically, the never-say-die attitude was rewarded with the final kick of the game when Howson struck a second to avoid extra-time and secure victory. The players immediately headed for the fans, but were quickly ushered from the field as Carlisle fans came pouring onto the pitch. Gary McAllister re-appeared on the touchline and the scenes in the dressing room were of unbridled joy and emotion. Carlisle United quickly agreed to McAllister's request to take his players back out to thank the fans and the scenes that followed will stay long in the memory of all who were there or witnessed them on TV. A line of stewards prevented the players from crossing the penalty box, but you could almost taste both the emotion and the respect between fans and players as the celebrations went on long into the night. Leeds United were not only going to Wembley, but were also on the verge of completing the most remarkable promotion in the history of the game.

RedKite

Left: **After Jonny Howson gave Leeds a first half lead, the whole team had to work hard to protect it.**

This page: **With the scores level at 2-2 on aggregate and extra-time looming Howson struck again to score a last minute winner that sent Leeds to the final at Wembley.**

Overleaf: **The win prompted scenes of unbridled joy among the Leeds fans on the terracing and the players on the pitch.**

AVID ALLE

LEEDS

HOWSON
14
OHS

BUILDING UP...

With tickets selling out in a matter of days and the city of Leeds buzzing about the prospect of a Wembley final, Gary McAllister was keen to isolate his players from the hype surrounding the Wembley clash with Doncaster Rovers. On the Tuesday before the game, the club held a media day at Thorp Arch where Jonny Howson proved a man in demand. The club even received a request from a local TV crew to film from the bedroom window of Howson's house to see if there was a glimpse of Elland Road. It was proper *Roy Of The Rovers* stuff and the young player took it all in his stride.

The media work was the squad's last act in Yorkshire before they headed off to a Hertfordshire hotel for three nights. Champneys Spa near Tring was a retreat in every sense of the word. Set in acres of grounds, the peace and quiet was deafening, and was only punctuated on the Friday evening when Frank Bruno's laughter could be heard booming around the corridors. Bruno used the hotel for his own training and his presence attracted the attention of a group of star-struck footballers who peeped through the gym windows with excitement.

The squad were preparing at Watford's training ground and had visited Wembley on the Friday lunchtime. The trip provided an early meeting with Doncaster as both teams arrived at the same time. There were nods of respect and a handful of players swapped pleasantries as they took pictures of the near-deserted Wembley. It was difficult to comprehend that the vast stadium would be nearly full in 48 hours time when the real action was due to begin. Doncaster manager Sean O'Driscoll cut a chilled figure as he surveyed the scene from the sidelines, and there was a brief chat with Gary McAllister before the two squads went their separate ways.

Back in Hertfordshire, there was one final press conference for McAllister and Dougie Freedman, and the players posed for pictures in their new suits. After training on the Saturday, it was into London for the final night of preparation. The Coca-Cola Championship Play-Off final was shown on the coach and the feeling towards Football League chairman Lord Mawhinney was clear when he met the teams of Bristol City and Hull City with murmurings from various parts of the bus. There followed the inevitable discussions about handshakes and possible trophy presentations, but contrary to suggestions from elsewhere there was nothing planned. A Marylebone hotel was the final stop-off point of a journey that had started back in Ireland the previous July. It had been a remarkable trip. And one that was to have an unpleasant final twist.

RedKite
POWERADE
Admiral
Coca-Cola

mitre

IT ALL ENDS IN TEARS

Ask any Leeds fan about a final appearance and they naturally fear the worst. Disappointment on such occasions is something we've all been born with and we're hardened to it. Yet it doesn't make it any easier to bear. Among the fans there was, if not an expectancy, certainly a belief that the team could win – and that was definitely mirrored in the dressing room. Having come so far, this was the big moment.

Around 50,000 Leeds fans turned Wembley into a bigger, vaster Elland Road, and the atmosphere was electric. When Mawhinney performed his pre-match ritual of meeting the teams, the viewers on TV saw a number of Leeds players offer their hand without making any eye contact and their feelings were clear.

Leeds recovered from a sticky opening and with the score 0-0 at half-time, there was a sense that the club's time had finally come. It hadn't. Doncaster scored early in the second period and held on for victory. At the final whistle, tears were shed in the stands and on the pitch. There were more tears in the dressing room and a feeling of hollowness among players and staff. Gary McAllister was devastated but put on a brave face when conducting his post-match duties. The players were consoled and cajoled, but there was no one to console or cajole the thousands of fans who headed back down Wembley Way. It had been a truly remarkable season, but the fairy tale had no happy ending.

Deep in the bowels of Wembley Stadium, though, Chapter Two was already being written. League One champion Andy Robinson had already pledged his future to the club before the Doncaster defeat, and chairman Ken Bates and Gary McAllister were already discussing the new season and planning for the club's future...

THE ARBITRATION SAGA

By Ken Bates

So much has been written about Leeds United's attempt to have the 15-point penalty overturned, much of which by people who haven't bothered to establish the facts, that it is worth setting the record straight. The recommendation of the arbitration panel is printed opposite.

When the club went into administration it forfeited its membership of the Football League, although this was suspended until the club's problems were resolved. At 5.15pm on Friday August 3 Leeds' membership was reinstated subject to a 15-point deduction. A condition of re-entry was that other than making representation to the other 71 clubs, no appeal was permitted and this condition was written into the agreement between the Football League and Leeds United. The club signed the agreement under duress. With only five working days before the start of the season, any further negotiations would have meant the end of Leeds United. Without permission to do so Leeds could not have fulfilled their opening fixture against Tranmere Rovers which under Football League rules, would have meant expulsion from the League. We were between a rock and a hard place.

The appeal to fellow clubs at a meeting held at the Churchill Hotel, Portland Square, London the following Thursday – just 48 hours before the season started – was a farce. The chairman of the meeting, Lord Mawhinney, who was also the League's chairman, presented the League's case, becoming in effect, counsel for the prosecution. So much for the chairman's impartiality. The jury consisted of the member clubs, all of whom had a vested interested in the outcome of the case because a 15-point deduction meant Leeds would be seriously disadvantaged against their competitors, the same people who would decide the outcome of the appeal. Subsequently, many clubs admitted that they voted out of self-interest rather than on the merits of the case.

Immediately following the result at this 'kangaroo court' – for in truth, that is what it was – we reviewed our options. The Football Association is the ultimate authority in English Football and the Football League is subject to the FA's rules. Accordingly, on August 30 we wrote to the FA asking them to review the League rules and procedures, and to inquire into whether the decision to deduct points was a decision that the Football League could properly take under its constitution and regulations. The reply, dated September 26, from Jonathan Hall, head of FA governance, said: "I do not feel it is therefore in any way appropriate for there to be any further enquiry into the decision made by the League on this matter."

On October 18, 2008 we wrote to Jonathan Hall again requesting him to understand the depth of feeling at the club and stated that our hope and expectation was that a commission of enquiry be set up. Our request was rejected on November 7.

Clearly, from the above, there was no justification for the criticism that Leeds United delayed matters.

The tribunal dismissed our appeal on the sole grounds that we had agreed not to appeal. That was the only argument put forward by the Football League in their case.

However, when Leeds issued their High Court writ, the League responded by saying the proper forum was arbitration. Surely, by doing so, they had waived that argument!

As a result, the League's rationale and explanation of what we did wrong was never examined. Just as well for the League because Lord Mawhinney was totally unable to tell the world of our "crime" when invited to do so live on Sky TV. Indeed, the League acknowledged we had done nothing wrong.

In addition to their judgement, the tribunal also recommended that any future dispute between a club and the League should be referred to an independent tribunal. Leeds promptly proposed a change of rule at the 2008 League AGM to reflect the recommendation. The League board opposed the changes and the lemmings who are members of the League supported the board. We now have a completely totalitarian organisation with no rights for the individual club.

Arbitration Report Postscript (Excerpt)

3. The Board should be astute not to think in terms of 'penalty' or a 'norm' as a starting point of whatever Condition is to be imposed. We are concerned that the Condition was described by the Board as a 'penalty' and was understandably perceived to be so.

4. We accept that the imposition of the 15 points in the instant case was not (and was not intended to be) a precedent, i.e. an automatic sanction in the absence of a CVA. Each case has to be assessed by the League having regard to the Club's individual circumstances leading up to and of the insolvency itself. Such Conditions as the League considers are required will reflect these circumstances and any merits the Club can establish.

5. We feel obliged to record that we consider an Appeal to Members of the League to be unsatisfactory. Some Clubs in the same League may not readily agree to reduce a points sanction in the understandable self-interest of their Clubs. We recommend:

1. That there should be an appeal to an Independent Tribunal;

2. In order to reduce uncertainty for the Club and other Clubs the Appeal process should be determined without delay. We suggest an Appeal should be lodged within 7 days of the decision and the decision of the Appeal body should be given within 21 days thereafter.